The Art of
Resin Jewelry

The Art of
Resin Jewelry

Layering, Casting, and
Mixed Media Techniques
for Creating Vintage
to Contemporary Designs

SHERRI HAAB

Watson-Guptill Publications | NEW YORK

First published in 2006 by
Watson-Guptill Publications,
Crown Publishing Group, a division of
Random House Inc., New York
www.crownpublishing.com
www.watsonguptill.com

All projects by Sherri Haab, unless otherwise noted.
All photography by Dan Haab, unless otherwise noted.

Paperback: ISBN-13: 978-0-8230-0344-0
         ISBN-10: 0-8230-0344-2
Paperback with DVD:
         ISBN-13: 978-0-8230-1502-3
         ISBN-10: 0-8230-1502-5

LIBRARY OF CONGRESS CATALOGING-IN-PUBLICATION DATA
Haab, Sherri.
 The art of resin jewelry : layering, casting, and
mixed media techniques for creating vintage to
contemporary designs / Sherri Haab.
   p. cm.
Includes index.
ISBN 0-8230-0344-2 (alk. paper)
1. Jewelry making. 2. Plastics craft. I. Title.
TT212.H32 2006
745.594'2--dc22
         2005028428

Senior Acquisitions Editor: Joy Aquilino
Editor: Michelle Bredeson
Designer: Alexandra Maldonado
Senior Production Manager: Ellen Greene

Manufactured in Malaysia

First printing, 2006

5 6 7 8 9 / 14 13 12 11 10

A NOTE TO READERS

When working with resins and other suggested products, readers are strongly cautioned to follow manufacturers' directions, to heed warnings, and to seek prompt medical attention for an injury. In addition, readers are advised to keep all potentially harmful supplies away from children.

To my husband, Dan, thank you for the great photographs and hours of hard work.

Thank you to my friends Jacqueline and Wendy for the fantastic projects and help with so many aspects of the book.

Thanks to the suppliers and manufacturers who supplied products and technical support.

And many thanks to the staff at Watson-Guptill for their dedication to the development and publication of this book.

contents

Introduction 8

The Basics 14
Types of Resin 16
Safety Guidelines & Equipment 19
Working with Resin 21
Colorants & Additives 25
Finishing Techniques 28
Jewelrymaking Basics 30

Using Resin as a Coating 34
Pressed Flower Bracelet 36
Cloisonné-Style Jewelry 40
Photo Collage Charm Bracelet 43

Casting with Ready-made Molds 46
Working with Preformed Molds 48
Bakelite-Style Bracelet 50
Fabric Pendant 54
Silver & Gold Leaf Jewelry 59
Retro Stretch Bracelet 63
Layered Elements Jewelry 66
Glitter Gem Bead Necklace 70
Candy Jewelry 74

Making Your Own Molds for Casting 78

Moldmaking Materials & Techniques   80
Faux Celluloid Bracelet   83
Pod Bead Bracelet   88
Faux Jade Neckpiece   92
Bangle Bracelets   96
Faux Amber Jewelry   101

Combining Resin with Polymer Clay 106

Working with Polymer Clay   108
Sequined Belt Buckle   109
Techno Polymer Clay Bezels   112
Funky Flower Pins   116
Faux Dichroic Glass Pendant   120
Polymer Clay Collage Pendant   122

Contributing Artists   125
Suppliers   126
Index   128

Introduction

When I think of resin, one of my earliest memories is of resin "grapes," a popular living room accessory from the 1970s, which were proudly displayed on my mother's coffee table.

You may also recall "clacker balls," a child's toy from the '70s, which consisted of a string with a resin ball at each end. Kids would whack them together to make noise, annoying a parent or anyone else within earshot. If you are old enough to remember clacker balls, no doubt you also remember seeing the lost ones hanging from power lines that crossed the road. Resin crafting for jewelry, using the same type of resin, was also popular back then. Clear resin cubes with natural specimens embedded were featured in craft magazines, along with other resin novelties such as key chains.

Today, there is a renewed interest in resin as a material for crafting jewelry. Contemporary resin designs are very sophisticated, and resin is used for many innovative applications. Ranging from crystal clear to translucent glowing hues, resin has a wonderful appeal for its glass-like properties. It can be used to simulate other materials or as an element in mixed-media designs. I am drawn to resin because it's a great way to add color to jewelry and it has the ability to encapsulate found or textured objects that might not otherwise be used as a jewelrymaking material. Candy, found objects, and even delicate flowers can all be embedded in resin as a jewelry design element.

Resin is a liquid plastic that becomes a solid following a chemical exothermic reaction. Heat

Stag Beetle Pendant by Charlie Hines. (Photo by artist.)

Yellow and Orange Resin Petal Necklace by Carla Edwards. Resin, gold leaf, paper, and oxidized silver. (Photo by artist.)

OPPOSITE Petal Necklace by Lulu Smith. (Photo by Douglas Yaple.)

is generated when a hardener or catalyst is introduced to a base resin, causing polymerization (linking of the polymers) of the plastic. The resin goes from a liquid state to a solid rigid form in this process, and remains as such.

New resin formulas, including low-odor products, are easy to mix and measure. There are a number of resin products on the market today, offering more options than were available in the past, making this an exciting craft to revisit or to discover for the first time. In writing this book my goal was to discover the easiest products to use, without the need for industrial equipment, vacuums, or scales. There are several types of resin, including epoxy, polyurethane, and polyester resins, that are used in jewelrymaking. All

of the projects in this book can be accomplished with simple supplies that are readily available from local craft and hobby stores.

Early plastics—predecessors to modern resins and plastics—included celluloid, which was developed in the mid-nineteenth century. Celluloid resembles ivory or horn and was used as a substitute for these natural materials. Bakelite plastic followed close behind, and was popular through the 1940s, especially during war time when metals and other jewelrymaking materials were scarce. During the 1960s and 1970s plastic remained popular as a jewelrymaking material, with even more synthetic types being developed. Each decade has seen innovative uses for plastic in jewelry design, making it an exciting

Rings by Renathe Schneider. (Photo by Dan Haab.)

Sea Shapes by Wendy Wallin Malinow. Cast resin, polymer clay, and rubber cord. (Photo by Dan Haab.)

Luna Bracelet by Lulu Smith. (Photo by Douglas Yaple.)

medium for jewelry designers. Especially with the rise in popularity of retro or vintage styles, renewed interest in and demand for plastic jewelry seems to have exploded.

Resin and plastic jewelry is often associated with inexpensive, mass-produced, costume jewelry found in discount department stores. However, you will discover that artists and designers often incorporate plastic and resin into the jewelry designs they sell to galleries and higher end stores. This doesn't make either category of jewelry any less valid, but rather illustrates that plastic jewelry has a wide range of appeal. Resin jewelry is often whimsical and colorful. Resin can be used in a variety of techniques and incorporated into mixed-media designs. Plastic jewelry that was considered dime-store jewelry in its day is now highly collectible, selling competitively with fine jewelry on Internet auction sites.

Resin crafting is similar to making candy. In candymaking, factors such as measuring, temperature, and timing need to be attended to with accuracy and precision to ensure success. Like candy, it's easy to create resin objects as long as you measure and mix accurately, use the proper materials, and follow safety recommendations.

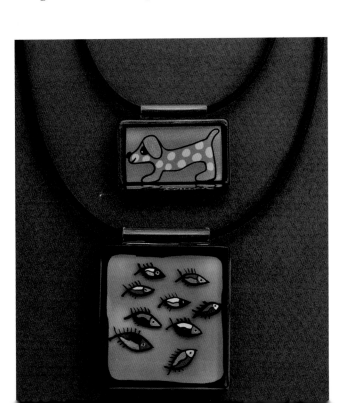

Dog and Aquarium Pendants by Renathe Schneider. (Photo by Dan Haab.)

Cherub Brooch by Robert Dancik. Epoxy resin, papier mâché pulp, PMC, sterling silver, pearl, and copper. (Photo by Douglas Foulke.)

Fire Rock Pendant by Robert Dancik. Epoxy resin, papier mâché pulp, and sterling silver. (Photo by Douglas Foulke.)

Resin is a multi-faceted craft. This book touches on techniques for working with different types of resin, moldmaking products, and many other jewelrymaking materials. In the first chapter, "The Basics," I discuss the different types of resin and their applications, as well as other supplies and techniques for working with resin. "Using Resin as a Coating" includes several projects for embedding images and other items in a glass-like coating. "Casting with Ready-made Molds" features techniques for crafting jewelry using molds made especially for resin, as well as candymaking and other purchased molds. In "Making Your Own Molds for Casting," you will learn how to form your own molds to create unique jewelry pieces. "Combining Resin with Polymer Clay" explores options for making mixed-media pieces using polymer clay. My goal is to give you a familiarity with resin and a variety of ideas for application.

It's exciting to see modern designers incorporating resin into new jewelry designs. Designs like the ones on these pages and throughout this book will give you a glimpse of the variety of effects possible when working with resin and will hopefully inspire you to create your own one-of-a-kind jewelry pieces.

OPPOSITE Spring Choker by Wendy Wallin Malinow. (Photo by Dan Haab.)

The Basics

Types of Resin

Resins used for jewelrymaking fall into several categories, each possessing unique qualities that make one type preferable to another for a certain application or technique. Epoxy, polyurethane, and polyester resins are described here. There are variations within these categories, including differences in mixing ratios, curing times, and viscosity. Once you familiarize yourself with the different formulations, it will be easy to determine the type you need for your design.

EPOXY RESIN

Epoxy resin is widely available and has a variety of applications. There are a number of subcategories of epoxy resin, including adhesives, coatings, and epoxy casting resin.

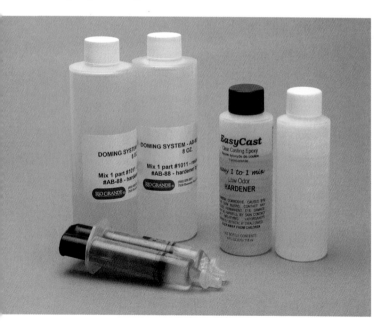

Epoxy resin and hardener is packaged in bottles for craft applications or in small tubes for use as an adhesive.

RIGHT Two-part epoxy resin adhesive should be mixed thoroughly on a nonabsorbent surface such as waxed paper or aluminum foil.

Epoxy resin adhesive is available at any hardware or craft store. The resin is a two-part system that is usually packaged in small, dual-tube dispensers. It is mixed thoroughly and then left to cure overnight, although some adhesives are quick-setting and take only minutes to cure. This type of resin is good for small applications, such as gluing on a pin back, or for making small repairs. Devcon 2-Ton® and Devcon 5-Minute® are two brands that are used in this book.

Epoxy coating resin is bottled in larger containers than the adhesive types and is sold in craft and hobby stores. It is formulated to be a pouring resin and is often less viscous and has a slower curing time than an epoxy resin adhesive, curing anywhere from overnight to a couple of days. The clear plastic coating you may have noticed on a wood table in a restaurant or bar is a common example of epoxy coating resin. It is durable and self-leveling, providing a smooth, clear, glass-like surface. Envirotex Lite® and Colores™ are two brands of epoxy coating resin that I use for the projects in this book.

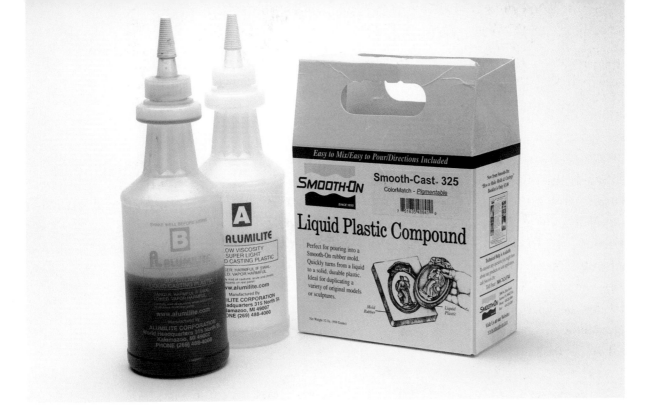

Alumilite and Smooth-Cast polyurethane resins are two examples of casting resins designed to mix easily with a 1:1 resin/hardener ratio.

For jewelry, epoxy coating resin can be used in many exciting ways. Clear resin looks like glass and can be used to protect pictures or small collage elements in a jewelry bezel. It can also be layered with other elements to create depth. Colored resins can be used to carefully fill the celled walls of a metal stamping and produce a faux cloisonné effect. Some artists apply colored resin to metal in a painterly fashion. Other artistic methods include mixing or embedding pigment powders, glitter, dried flowers, and other small objects in epoxy coating resin. Imitative techniques can be achieved by simply adding fillers and certain pigments to change the characteristics of the resin. The design possibilities are endless.

Epoxy casting resin can be cast into molds to make dimensional forms. Environmental Technology (ETI) has a product called EasyCast®,

which is a clear epoxy formulated especially for casting. This type of epoxy casting resin is a bit easier to use than other casting formulas (see below) because it allows you more time to work before it sets up (thickens) or cures (hardens). The extra time allows you to release air bubbles from the resin by using a heat gun over the surface. There are limitations on how large a piece you can cast, but for most projects, this is not an issue since jewelry pieces are generally small.

POLYURETHANE CASTING RESIN

Polyurethane, or "urethane," resin is a general-purpose casting resin, commonly used to make miniatures and figurines. This resin is generally formulated to cure quickly, anywhere from two to twenty minutes—although a few types cure more slowly. Urethane casting resin is available in a transparent amber tint, to which colorants and fillers can be added. It is also available in white, ivory, and black. Concentrated colors formulated especially for resin are sold as companion products to tint and color polyurethane resin. This resin is especially sensitive to moisture, so adding other types of coloring agents, such as artist's pastels (which absorb humidity), may inhibit curing. This type of resin works especially well for casting larger or detailed sculptural pieces in rigid or flexible rubber silicone molds. The projects in this book call for Alumilite or Smooth-Cast™ brand resins.

POLYESTER CASTING RESIN

This resin has the ability to produce crystal-clear castings, and to remain consistently clear through large or thick pieces. The finished resin castings are very strong and resemble glass. Instead of the equal mixing ratios common to other types of resin, polyester resin is activated by adding a very small amount of catalyst to the resin. Because the amount of catalyst added is very small in relation to the resin, measuring needs to be especially accurate for a successful casting. Too much catalyst can overheat the resin and crack it; too little will leave the resin tacky. Dyes and pigments are sold as companion products and can be added to this type of resin to tint or color it.

Extra care must be taken when using polyester resin as the chemicals are quite toxic and very harmful to your health if you do not use proper safety and ventilation equipment.

The projects in this book do not involve the use of polyester resin, but it can be used in place of other resins to make similar finished pieces. Read all Material Safety Data Sheets (MSDS) before beginning a project.

Confetti Heart Pendant by Wendy Wallin Malinow. The layered elements jewelry project on page 66 has instructions for embedding objects and other elements in cast pieces.

WHICH RESIN SHOULD YOU USE?

Different resins have specific requirements for mixing and measuring depending on the type and brand, and some work better for certain applications than others. For each project in this book, I suggest a particular type or brand of resin to use, and give directions specific to that resin. If you choose to use a different type or brand, make sure you follow the manufacturer's instructions for that product.

Safety Guidelines & Equipment

Resin is safe and easy to use as long as you follow general safety guidelines. Protective gear should be used with all types of resin, and you should become familiar with and follow handling instructions provided by the manufacturer of the product you are using. Remember that just because a certain type of resin is low-odor, that does not mean there are no fumes. Invest in safety equipment and keep it close at hand. Don't be intimidated by the use of respirators or gloves; it will give you peace of mind to know that you are protecting your health.

BASIC SAFETY MEASURES

Read the Material Safety Data Sheet (MSDS) that accompanies the product you are using. If it's not packaged with the product, you can request a copy from the company or possibly view it on their Web site. This sheet gives you the technical properties of the material, as well as safe handling and first aid information.

Most importantly, you should work in a well-ventilated area when using resin materials. An exhaust fan and open windows and doors will increase air circulation and keep fumes from collecting as you work. Keep your workroom away from eating and main living areas for another measure of respiratory safety. A respirator will provide protection from harmful vapors and should always be worn as you prepare and mix resin.

Never pour resin, shavings, or moldmaking materials down the drain, as they are harmful to the environment. Follow the proper disposal methods recommended by the manufacturer or check with local authorities to ensure that the resin is properly contained before disposing. Also, remember to keep all resin materials and tools away from food preparation areas.

IMPORTANT EQUIPMENT

Here is a list of safety equipment and supplies needed when working with resin or other art materials mentioned in the book:

A respirator that is approved by the National Institute for Occupational Safety and Health (NIOSH) is a necessity. You can find respirators in hardware or paint stores. Use the filters designed for fumes, rather than dust filters meant for larger particulates. Always wear a respirator when working with resin, hardeners, and moldmaking liquids.

Disposable gloves should be worn to protect your skin as prolonged or repeated contact with resin can cause sensitivity and irritation. Protective gloves made of nitrile or butyl, which are synthetic elastic materials, are the best types to use. Other types of rubber gloves may allow the resin to penetrate the glove. If you get resin on your skin, wash it off quickly with soap and water and follow the guidelines on the MSDS sheet accompanying the product.

Barrier cream is a lotion for your hands that can be used as an extra precaution to protect your skin. It will help to keep the resin from sticking to your skin. Do not use this as a substitute for gloves however. Barrier cream can be purchased at art supply stores and pharmacies.

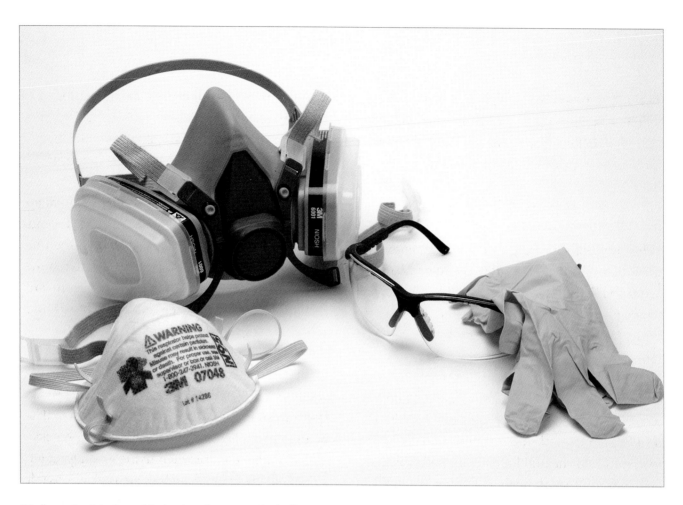

It's important to invest in basic safety gear, including a respirator, dust mask, protective eye wear, and gloves.

Eye goggles or glasses will protect your eyes while you are working with resin and hardeners. No matter how careful you are, a drop of resin can splat toward your eye when you least expect it. Protective eyewear can be found at hardware stores or purchased online.

A dust mask should always be worn when sanding or drilling resin. You should also use a dust mask when adding powdered fillers or pigments to resin, as the airborne particulates are harmful to your lungs. Disposable dust masks from a hardware or paint store are sufficient.

Working with Resin

This section introduces basic materials and techniques you will need to make every project in this book. Familiarize yourself with them and refer back to this section while working.

SETTING UP A WORKING ENVIRONMENT

When arranging an area to work in, the most important consideration is that the room be well-ventilated. Exhaust fans are ideal, but opening a window to create air flow will also help to keep the fumes to a minimum. Work at room temperature (about 72°F or warmer), as cooler temperatures inhibit curing. Make sure your work area is set up with everything you need close at hand. Keep the area clear of obstacles that might cause spills or accidents. A layer of waxed paper or plastic on your work surface is helpful for catching spills, as the resin will not soak through and ruin a tabletop.

BASIC SUPPLIES

A few basic supplies are needed when working with resin. These items are often sold in kit form with resin components, so that you have everything you need to get started on a project.

Plastic mixing cups marked with units of volume are essential for mixing resin. The cups I prefer are made for Colores brand resin. These plastic cups are the perfect size for mixing small batches of resin and are clearly marked in different units of measure. The nice thing about purchasing plastic cups from the manufacturer of a resin product is that you know they will be compatible and nonreactive for use with the resin. Plastics such as polypropylene, polyethylene, and PVC will not react with resin. Do not use cups made of Styrofoam or other types of plastic as they will react when in contact with resin. Paper cups coated with wax are not a good choice either as the wax may flake off into the resin.

Plastic squeeze bottles with narrow tips are helpful to use when resin is needed to fill a confined space. Resin can be transferred to the bottle after mixing and neatly squeezed through the tip into small molds. Fine-tipped applicators are available to apply tiny amounts of resin with precision to areas requiring fine detail.

Stir sticks, such as wooden craft sticks, chopsticks, or plastic straws are needed to mix resin. Use a fresh stick for each batch. A stick can also be used to apply resin. Small pointed toothpicks give you more control when trying to apply small amounts of resin or for tighter areas. A disposable paintbrush can also be useful for applying resin.

Waxed paper is a great surface to work on as resin will not soak in or stick to it. Use waxed paper under projects to collect drips, or as a surface to mix small amounts of resin into a palette of colors. If resin dries on the paper, it will simply peel away, leaving cured pieces of resin that could be salvaged to use as decorative elements to embed in future resin projects.

Paper towels, especially heavy ones sold as disposable shop towels in auto supply stores, are great for wiping the sides of bottles or collecting spills. If you accidentally overfill a mold, simply dip the corner of a paper towel into the mold and soak up the excess. This is easier and less messy than trying to pour excess resin out of the mold.

MEASURING AND MIXING TECHNIQUES

Accurate measuring and mixing are critical for resin to cure properly. The resins used in the projects in this book were chosen because they can be measured easily by volume (e.g., one part resin to one part hardener). The resin is measured by pouring each component into graduated mixing cups and carefully filling them according to the markings indicated for ounces, teaspoons, or cubic centimeters on the cup. Polyester resin, which is not used in this book, can also be mixed using volume; follow the manufacturer's calculations for the number of drops of catalyst needed for a certain volume of resin. Other types of resin not covered in this book require a scale for more accurate measuring.

Follow the method below for most epoxy and polyurethane resins with a longer pot life. The pot life is the amount of time you have to work before the resin starts to set up and thicken. For quick-setting resins, you will not have time to transfer to another cup; make sure you mix well and then quickly pour your resin before it sets up. As each resin formulation varies, it's best to read all of the directions provided by the manufacturer before beginning your project. Some types of resin, for example, require that colorants or fillers be added to one part before mixing the components together.

A word of caution: Always mix the proper ratios recommended to avoid overheating the resin and causing it to pop or splat.

1. To mix resin with hardener, measure the resin component into one cup and the hardener into another, following the proper ratio. This photo shows a 1:1 ratio. Most manufacturers recommend that you avoid mixing small amounts (less than ¼ ounce of each component) to ensure success.

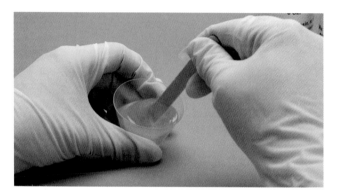

2. Pour the hardener into the resin, scraping the cup well to maintain the proper ratio. Stir well to incorporate the resin and hardener. As you stir, scrape the sides without whipping, as whipping or folding will cause more air bubbles to form.

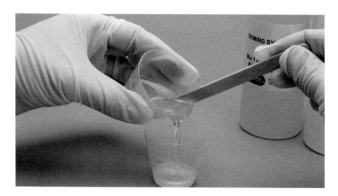

3. Pour the mixture into a clean cup and mix again briefly. The transfer of cups and second stirring will ensure that the resin is completely incorporated with the hardener, so that the resin will cure properly and not become tacky later on.

GETTING RID OF AIR BUBBLES

After mixing your resin and pouring it into molds or applying it to a surface, you will notice air bubbles in the resin. No matter how careful you are to avoid them during mixing or pouring, a few are always present. They need to be removed before the resin cures, unless you want to intentionally leave them in your design. Many of the bubbles will dissipate on their own as the resin sits, especially with slower curing resins. However, if you wait too long, the resin will start to thicken and the bubbles will be almost impossible to remove, making timing an important factor in removing bubbles. With experience, you will become familiar with the timing needed to remove bubbles. Quick-setting formulas give you little or no time to remove bubbles, but are often OK as the bubbles mostly tend to dissipate on their own.

Modelmakers and production jewelry designers use vacuum chambers to remove bubbles, but there are ways around using one if you don't want to invest in this type of equipment. To remove air bubbles manually from uncured resin, you can heat the surface of the resin. The easiest method I know of is to use a heat gun, which is sold in craft and rubber stamping stores. Do not use a hair dryer in place of a heat gun. Although it looks similar to a heat gun, it will blow the resin and make a mess.

A heat gun's primary purpose is to *heat,* not to blow, air. This method was shared by Marie Browning from ETI and was used for the projects in the book. Hold the heat gun over the liquid resin a short distance away for a brief time to remove the air bubbles. You can see them dissipate quickly. It's best to run the heat over the resin with a few short passes rather than holding it over continuously for a long time. You don't want to risk overheating the molds, paper inclusions, or other elements that might be damaged

A heat gun commonly used for melting embossing powders for rubber stamping is a helpful tool to remove the air bubbles from uncured resin.

by heat. Be cautious not to hold the gun at an angle where you might blow the resin, causing it to splash out of the mold or off of the surface you are coating. Check the resin after 5 to 10 minutes and repeat the process if any bubbles remain.

CURING RESIN

Warm temperatures are essential for curing resin. After working at room temperature to mix the resin, move the resin to a place where it can remain undisturbed for the specified curing time. Resin will cure at room temperature, but you can speed the process by curing it under a low-watt light bulb. A 60- to 100-watt bulb will generate enough heat to hasten curing. Several manufactures offer instructions for building a light box where you can set your pieces to cure in a warm protected environment. The warmth of the sun works equally well. The important thing is to keep the piece in a warm, draft-free environment while it cures.

Resin is fully cured when it is not tacky and feels hard to the touch. You can test it with a toothpick to avoid getting a fingerprint on the surface. Curing times vary widely depending on many factors, such as the type of resin used, the particular brand, the amount used, and the temperature during mixing and curing.

TROUBLESHOOTING

It's a good idea to start with a few simple projects to become familiar with the properties of the resin you are working with. Most resin manufacturers have helpful information on Web sites or technicians you can reach by phone or e-mail. It's likely that other customers have had the same questions that the company can answer quickly for you. Here are a few of the most common problems you might encounter when working with resin.

Problem	Cause
Resin remains sticky or tacky after curing.	Resin was mixed improperly or incorrect mixing ratio was used.
Resin remains soft or flexible after curing.	Too much colorant or dye was mixed into resin.
Tiny bubbles create cloudiness.	Resin was too cold when mixed.
Bubbles trapped under embedded objects.	Object should have been brushed with resin before placing into liquid resin layer. Push on the back of the object with a toothpick to release the air after it is embedded.
Paper or other inclusions turn clear or change color.	Item was not sealed properly before adding to resin. Use decoupage glue or acrylic spray to seal paper and other porous objects.
Resin sticks in mold.	Mold should have been treated with release spray prior to use or resin needs to cure longer. Try placing mold in a refrigerator for a few minutes before removing pieces.
Resin becomes tacky over time.	Moisture or a noncompatible substance is reacting with the resin. Make sure all of your embedded items are oil- and moisture-free.

Colorants & Additives

Art materials including pigment powders, glitters, and gold leaf are a few possibilities for adding color and texture to resin. As long as the additive or colorant is nonreactive with the resin you are using, anything goes. Along with adding materials to mix with uncured resin, you can apply acrylic paint, permanent pen, or colored pencil to layers of cured resin. Make sure these mediums are thoroughly dry before adding more resin. Add a final layer of resin to seal the color.

COLOR

Color is bold and exciting when added to resin. You have a few options for coloring resin. You can add opaque pigments to achieve a solid color or add just a small amount of dye to tint transparent resin. With a little experimentation you will find favorite color combinations and effects you can create by adding a certain colorant to your resin.

Liquid pigments are available from resin manufacturers and are designed to be compatible with the products they sell. The colors can be mixed to create a variety of hues from transparent to opaque. As a general rule, most are very concentrated and it may take only a small drop of pigment to color an entire batch of resin. Start with a small amount on a toothpick and add more until you achieve the desired hue. If you add too much color the final product may remain soft and flexible, so use just the minimum amount to get the color you want.

Powdered pigments are sold through art suppliers to be used for mixing egg tempera, watercolor, acrylic, and other paints. They can also be

Pigments, dyes, pastels, and iridescent powders are used to add color and texture to resin.

used as additives for resin. The pigment will color the resin and also add texture as some pigments are ground less fine than others. Pearl Ex powders by Jacquard are finely ground pigments, sold individually or in economical sets. These powders come in shimmering colors that create beautiful effects when mixed with resin. They can be combined to create custom colors as well. Be sure to wear a dust mask at all times when working with pigment powder, as it can damage your lungs if inhaled.

Polyurethane resins are sensitive to moisture. Since moisture can be absorbed by dry pigments, it's better to stick with liquid pigments made especially for polyurethane resin products.

Artist's pastels are available at a low cost and come in a variety of colors. Make sure you use soft, not oil, pastels. To add pastels to resin, use the blade of a knife to scrape or shave the side of a pastel stick into the resin, mixing until the desired color is achieved. Pastels will absorb moisture in the air similarly to pigment powders, especially in humid climates. Keep this in mind when working with polyurethane resin, which is sensitive to moisture as mentioned in the section above on working with powdered pigments.

You can mix an endless variety of hues by adding colorants to resin.

INCLUSIONS AND FILLERS

Half the fun of working with resin is adding materials to suspend in the resin. There are a variety of materials that can be added, as long as the items are completely free of moisture and do not contain materials that will react with the resin over time. Some artists embed natural specimens (bugs, butterflies, plants, etc.) into resin, processing them to remove any moisture before adding them to the resin. You can dry your own leaves and flowers by placing them between craft paper or the pages of an old phone book and leaving them to dry for several weeks. The projects in this book will give you lots of ideas for embellishments to embed in resin. No doubt you will be able to come up with your own unique materials to try.

Collage Pendants by Wendy Wallin Malinow. You can add anything from glitter to photographs to three-dimensional objects to liquid resin. See the layered elements project on page 66 for instructions.

RESIN MIX-INS

Here is a list of materials that can be added to resin, either as a decorative element or to change the texture of the resin. Lighter inclusions, such as glitter and metal leaf can be added when the resin is still in a liquid form. Heavier inclusions may sink to the bottom, so it's better to wait until the resin has become a bit firmer.

- Glitter
- Crushed glass
- Mica
- Metal leaf
- Dried flowers and other dried plants
- Sand and seashells
- Paper and fabric
- Small 3-D objects
- Game pieces
- Chips of dried resin
- Granite powder
- Beads
- Candy
- Popcorn
- Metal powder
- Threads and fibers
- Baked polymer clay pieces
- Porcelain powder

Finishing Techniques

After resin is fully cured, you can refine the surface or edges by drilling, sanding, or polishing. When sanding or drilling, be sure to wear a disposable dust mask to avoid breathing fine particles, which might harm your lungs.

SANDING

To remove rough edges or large imperfections on a resin piece, begin with a coarse grit of sandpaper (100 or 180 grit). Beauty salons carry nail files with both grits; they are ideal for removing the ridge left around a resin shape after removing it from a mold. Look for one that can be washed in water to remove the particles that build up on the file. Rinse the nail file after use. For the first step, when you are removing the larger bits of resin, you can work with dry sandpaper.

After you have removed most of the rough spots, sand with finer grits of paper. Sanding under water with wet/dry sandpapers keeps the dust to a minimum, and also serves to keep the particles from redepositing back onto the resin, which can lead to white spots in the resin that are difficult to remove. Fill the bottom of a shallow container dedicated for sanding resin (don't use it as a food container in the future). Change the water frequently when it becomes clouded with residue.

Continue to sand the edges of the piece under water using progressively finer papers until you are satisfied with the surface of the resin. After working with 100- or 180-grit papers,

move to 320-, 400-, 600-, and then to 800-grit papers. If you wish to refine further, continue sanding with the same method using 1000-, 1200-, and 1500-grit paper. These finer grits are available from auto supply stores.

As a final step, buff the sanded areas with wax using a soft cloth or disposable shop towel for a smooth shine. A small amount of carnauba wax (available at auto supply stores) buffed onto the resin will fill and conceal any fine scratches remaining. Buffing can also be accomplished by machine, as long as you use a variable speed machine. Faster speeds will heat the resin and cause small particles to melt back onto the resin and form a white residue.

Sanding supplies include nail files, sanding papers, buffing cloths, and car wax.

Sand resin pieces underwater and check periodically to make sure the residue is rinsed out of the paper to avoid redepositing shavings as you sand.

A pin vise or hand drill can be used to drill easily through a cured resin piece.

DRILLING

Drill holes in resin after it has fully cured. You can choose to drill before or after sanding the piece. Drill holes with a drill press or by hand using a hand drill or pin vise. Make sure you drill at a slow speed, even with a hand drill, as the resin will heat up and melt onto the bit at high speeds. The drilled holes can be cleaned out with a needle tool (used by ceramic artists) or drill bit until the hole is clear of shavings.

There are a few things you can do to drill more easily and accurately. A drill press will keep the bit in a fixed position so you can concentrate on holding the resin piece in place. If you do not have access to a drill press, you can place the resin piece in a vise to hold it stable as you drill. A piece of leather placed in the vise will keep the resin from becoming scratched. Small beads or holes can be drilled using a pin vise, holding the resin bead in one hand and drilling with the other. You will find that your fingers can sense the pressure of the bit, affording you some control over the accuracy of the direction you are drilling. Save your rejected resin pieces to practice drilling through; this may save you from ruining your favorite pieces later on.

If you make a mistake and accidentally drill through the back of a piece, for example, you can fill the hole with more resin, let it cure, and drill again. A little epoxy resin adhesive is often all that is needed to fix drilling mistakes.

Jewelrymaking Basics

For the most part, all the techniques you need to make a project in this book are included in the directions. However, there are some basic jewelrymaking materials and techniques that are helpful to know about before you get started.

TOOLS

A few simple jewelrymaking tools are essential for creating professional-looking jewelry designs.

Jeweler's pliers will make a big difference in the quality of your work. Here are the basic pliers you will need for some projects in this book. *Needle-nose pliers* are common household pliers that have long tapered jaws with teeth. *Chain-nose pliers* are used to open and close jump rings. They are also useful for gripping or holding wire or for crimping down the ends of a wire wrap. These are similar to needle-nose pliers, but do not have teeth. *Round-nose pliers* are essential for forming wire loops. They have graduated tips for

making loops of various sizes. *Flat-nose pliers* are useful for holding or gripping wire. You can also use them to bend wire into a 90-degree angle with ease. *Crimping pliers* are specialized pliers that are used to pinch the center of crimp beads and secure them to nylon-coated wire.

Wire cutters will cut wire cleanly. An old pair of wire cutters or a heavy-duty pair from the hardware store is helpful to have for cutting heavy-gauge wire, so you don't dull your good pair of wire cutters.

A needle tool can be used as a scriber, to make holes in clay or other soft materials, or to clean out holes after drilling.

Tweezers are useful for positioning small beads or rhinestones while gluing them in place or setting them in resin. Tweezers are also great for holding beading cord to make tight knots.

Various types of pliers. Clockwise from top left: crimping pliers, chain-nose pliers, flat-nose pliers, needle-nose pliers, round-nose pliers, and wire cutters.

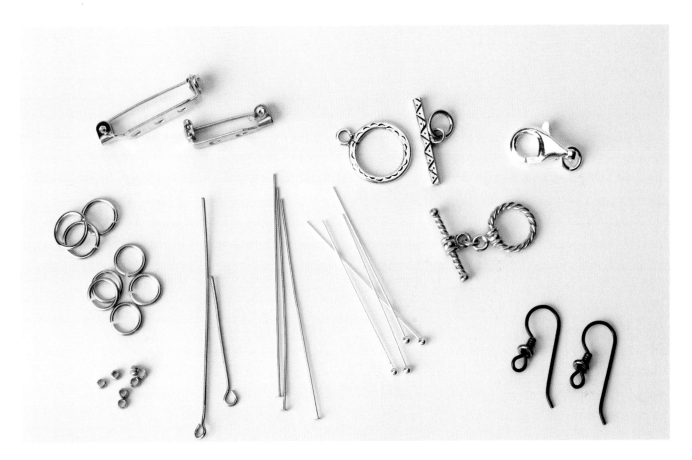

FINDINGS

Finishing a piece of jewelry is sometimes the most important step in the process of creating it. You want a piece that will hold up and look professional at the same time. The right findings—the metal components that hold a piece of jewelry together—can really enhance a piece.

Choose findings that complement the resin elements or other components in the piece. Beading supply shops, craft stores, and catalogs sell a variety of findings for making jewelry. The findings listed here are commonly used in jewelrymaking.

Jump rings are small metal loops that are used to link components together. Jump rings are available in fine or base metal.

Findings are the hardware you need to pull your jewelry designs together. Clockwise from top left: Pin backs, loop-and-toggle clasps, lobster claw clasp, ear wires, silver head pins, brass head pins, eye pins, crimp beads, and jump rings.

Ear wires are available in a variety of styles and metal finishes. Use jump rings or leave holes in your piece to attach purchased ear wires.

Head pins are short wires with a ball or flat pad on one end. You can hang a bead on a head pin and then coil the pin's top to make a loop for hanging.

Eye pins are similar to head pins, except they have a loop instead of a ball at the bottom. This allows you to hang another piece or bead from the loop.

Pin backs can be glued to the back of a pin with epoxy, or some pin backs come with ready-to-use adhesive strips. They are sold in different sizes and styles. Pin backs are usually available in base metal or sterling silver.

Clasps are closures used to join the ends of a necklace or bracelet together. Loop-and-toggle, lobster claw, spring ring, hook-and-eye, and barrel are all types of clasps that are available commercially. Clasps can really add to your overall design, so choose a clasp that complements your piece in style and weight.

Crimp beads are tiny beads used to secure the end of nylon-coated wire. Crimp beads can also be used to hide knots on the ends of cord for a neat finish. If used on cord, they can simply be glued over the knot or flattened over the knot with a pair of flat-nose pliers.

Bead tips are used to cover knots when stringing with thread. Bead tips have two cups, like a clamshell, that close together to hide the knot and a hook that attaches to a jump ring or clasp. To help secure the knot, apply a drop of glue to it before closing the bead tip.

Jump rings are small metal loops that are used to link components together. Jump rings are available in fine or base metal and come in different diameters and thicknesses.

Do *open jump rings by twisting the ends out to each side with pliers. Close jump rings in the same fashion by bringing the ends back in from the sides.*

Don't *pull jump rings open and apart. This weakens them by adding stress to the metal.*

WRAPPING WIRE LOOPS

Wire wrapping is a fundamental jewelrymaking skill that is used in a number of projects in this book. Once you get the hang of making loops and wrapping wire, you can use this skill to combine any type of bead with silver, gold, or colored wire. Here's how you do it:

1. Bend the wire toward you at a 90-degree angle with chain-nose or flat-nose pliers.

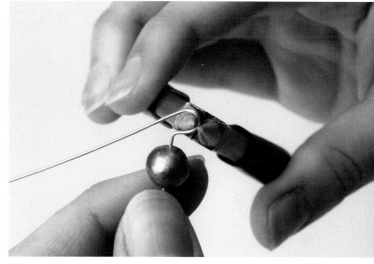

2. Switch to round-nose pliers and wrap the wire around the pliers away from you to form a loop.

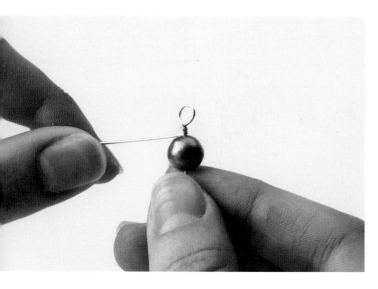

3. Wrap the wire around the base of the loop several times to secure. Clip off the excess wire. Use the tip of the chain-nose pliers to pinch the end of the wire down.

4. If you would like to join wire-wrapped beads together, string a bead onto the wire and make a wrapped loop at the other end. Repeat steps 1 through 3, wrapping close to the bead.

Using Resin
as a Coating

Pressed Flower Bracelet

PRESERVE REAL FLOWERS, leaves, and other botanicals in resin to make colorful jewelry. Make sure plants are perfectly dry before layering them in resin. Plant oils can interfere with curing if they remain in the flower. You can press your own flowers or buy them commercially dried from a craft or hobby store.

To make one bracelet, you will need:

Open bezel bracelet (Eastern Findings: #7187)

Colores bright opaque resin and hardener (thin)

Small pressed flowers (Nature's Pressed)

Decoupage glue (Mod Podge®)

Envirotex Lite epoxy resin

1. Mix a small batch of Colores resin (at least 1 teaspoon colored resin to ½ teaspoon hardener). Mix thoroughly with a stirring stick. This resin gives you plenty of working time (at least an hour), so don't worry about having to rush before the resin sets up.

Set the bracelet on a level surface with waxed paper or an old magazine underneath. Use a craft stick to coat the bottom of each bezel with a thin layer of resin.

Let the resin cure in a warm place, undisturbed. This may take 24 hours or longer.

2. To add the pressed flowers, brush a small amount of decoupage glue onto the surface of the resin.

3. Use tweezers to place the flower in the center of the bezel while the glue is still wet, and press to adhere.

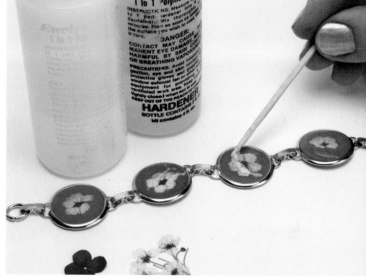

4. Carefully brush a layer of glue over the flower and let it dry thoroughly before covering with resin. The glue seals the flower as some darker flowers will "bleed" color into the resin; lighter petals tend to go transparent.

5. Mix up a small batch of clear Envirotex Lite resin. Use a toothpick to cover the flower with more resin. Let the resin cure in a warm place. Make sure the resin is very hard and fully cured before wearing the bracelet.

FLOWER EARRINGS

To make earrings, coat the bottom of the bezels with colored resin as in step 1 of the flower bracelet. Add small flowers and coat with clear resin as directed in steps 2 through 5. Let the resin cure for several days in a warm place before assembling the earrings.

To make one pair of earrings, you will need:

Materials for pressed flower bracelet (except open bezel bracelet)

Two open bezels (Eastern Findings)

Two $\frac{1}{16}$"-long micro eyelets

Two ear wires

Two pieces of wire

Two beads

1. Use a hand drill with a small drill bit to make a hole at the top of the bezel for hanging. You can add a hole at the bottom if you want to add a dangle. Place an eyelet in the hole.

2. Set the eyelet with an eyelet setter and a hammer. Be sure to tap on the back side of the bezel to avoid scratching the resin.

Use a piece of wire to form a loop to attach the earrings to ear wires. The pair shown has a bead added to the wire before forming the loop. You can simply attach the earrings to ear wires with jump rings if you don't want to add beads.

Cloisonné-Style Jewelry

CLOISONNÉ IS AN ENAMELING technique in which thin walls of wire separate areas of colored enamel to form a design. In this project, resin is used to simulate the look of traditional glass enamel. Die-cut metal shapes stamped with relief patterns make wonderful metal bases on which to paint with colored resin. Thin resin will flow and fill the walled cells in a stamping. Resin mixed with thick hardener will allow you to apply the colored resin on a domed or flat surface for a more painterly style. For this project I used thin hardener.

To make one necklace or several pins, you will need:

Brass butterfly stampings (Eastern Findings)

Colores clear epoxy resin with thick or thin hardener depending on stamping

Powdered pigments (Pearl Ex)

Waxed paper and toothpicks

Flat-backed rhinestones (optional)

Devcon 2-Ton epoxy adhesive

Pin back finding (for pin)

Chain, jump rings, beads, and head pins (for necklace)

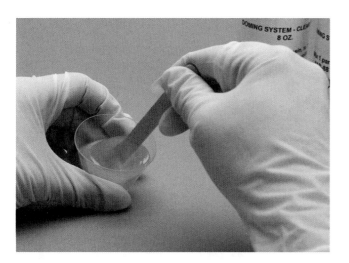

1. Clean any residue or oils off of the stamping with soap and water; dry thoroughly. Set the stamping on a level working surface.

   Mix a small batch of resin: at least 1 teaspoon resin to ½ teaspoon thick or thin hardener. This resin gives you plenty of working time (at least an hour), so don't worry about having to rush before the resin sets up.

2. To add color to the resin, drop a small amount of the mixed resin onto a piece of waxed paper. Use a toothpick to stir in powdered pigments.

3. Use the point of a toothpick or a pin (for tight areas) to apply the colored resin into the cells of the stamping. You can also use the fine-tipped syringes available in the Colores kit. If you accidentally overfill a cell, dip the corner of a paper towel into it to absorb the excess resin.

Let the pieces cure in a warm place for 24 hours or longer until the resin is hard.

4. If you like, you can place rhinestones in the resin while it is still liquid.

To make a pin, use epoxy adhesive to glue a pin back on the back of the stamping. Let the epoxy cure.

To make a necklace, hang the finished butterflies from a purchased chain using jump rings. Use head pins to add accent beads to the chain to finish.

The purple butterfly on the left was covered with thick resin in several colors. A toothpick was drawn through the resin to move the color around and to distribute it evenly on the surface of the stamping.

Photo Collage Charm Bracelet

TINY FRAMES CAPTURE PHOTOS and ephemera from the past to make personal memento bracelets. Fabric scraps, old buttons, pressed flowers, even a lock of hair add interest to the tiny collages. This bracelet makes a precious gift for Mother's day, a baby shower, or a birthday.

Some printed materials need to be sealed before applying a resin coating. I seal most of the paper images I use with decoupage glue, letting them dry thoroughly before applying resin. Choose matte or photocopied images as some glossy photos printed with an ink-jet printer will "bleed" when water-based glue is applied to seal the photo.

To make one bracelet, you will need:

Assorted bezels (Blue Moon Beads or Build-A-Bezel Charms by Karen Foster Designs)

Envirotex Lite epoxy resin

Assorted collage papers, miniature photos, or other printed material

Found objects, buttons, glitter, and rhinestones

Pressed flowers (Nature's Pressed)

Decoupage glue (Mod Podge)

Word charms (Blue Moon Beads)

Bracelet chain with toggle clasp

Jump rings

Assorted beads and charms

Head pins to attach beads

1. To create your own collage insert for each frame, remove the inserts from the purchased bezels. Use the clear plastic insert as a template or pattern for your insert. (Build-A-Bezel Charms include vellum patterns to place over an image for accurate cutting.) Choose a background paper or photo and trace around the insert.

2. Cut out the finished paper insert and coat the top surface and edges with decoupage glue. Let the glue dry.

3. Brush a layer of glue inside the frame. Slip the tiny insert into the bezel. You may have to bend it slightly. Use a craft knife to push the corners and sides down into the frame.

Layer other small bits of paper to create a collage using decoupage or white glue to adhere. Add 3-D embellishments to decorate the collage in the frame. Let the glue dry thoroughly.

4. Mix a small batch of epoxy resin. Coat each collage to fill the frame using a stir stick. Let the epoxy cure before assembling the bracelet; this may take overnight or longer.

To assemble the bracelet, attach the frames to a purchased charm bracelet with jump rings.

You can add beads to head pins to make dangles. Word charms were added to the silver charm bracelet pictured on page 43 as an accent to the design.

For these pendants and pin, images cut from vintage magazines were layered in resin along with text printed on transparency film. Transparencies give you the effect of text or images that appear to be floating without a background in the resin.

Casting with Ready-made Molds

WORKING WITH PREFORMED MOLDS

One of the wonderful things about using resin as a jewelrymaking material is that it can be cast into three-dimensional forms. Preformed resin molds made from plastics such as polypropylene or polyethylene are sold specifically for casting dimensional shapes in resin. Other types of molds, such as ice-cube trays or rubber molds for candy-making, can be used as molds for resin as well if they are made with rubber or plastic that will not stick or react to the resin. Plastic candy molds made for suckers and chocolates will not work well with resin, because the resin sticks to the plastic; the rubber ones made for mints work best. When in doubt, test a small amount of resin on the back of the mold.

Some types of molds are better suited than others for certain conditions, such as the type of resin used, shape of the casting, etc. Flexible molds give you the ability to work with undercuts (intricate details) and sculptural forms that might not otherwise release easily from a rigid mold. Molds sold specifically for resin casting are simple and do not have undercuts that might otherwise make it difficult to remove your casting.

Release agents help keep the resin from sticking to the mold. They can be applied to condition the mold prior to use, by spraying or brushing the product onto the molds and then letting it dry before pouring the resin. It's a good idea to test your mold if you are worried about the resin

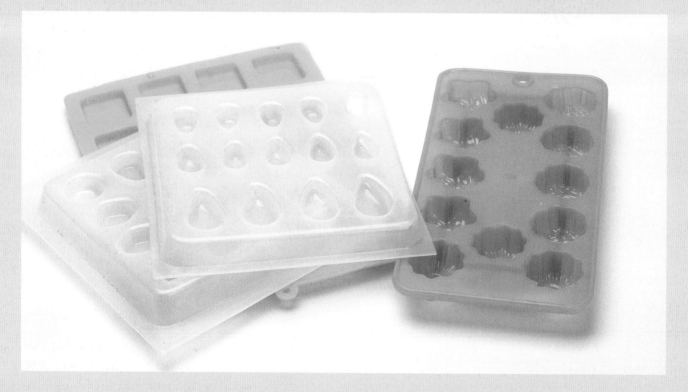

Purchased molds you can use include resin molds, ice-cube trays, and rubber candy molds.

sticking to it. To test the mold, turn it over and apply a small amount of resin to the back of the mold. This will allow you to test the mold without ruining the mold cavities.

To use a resin mold, condition the mold with mold release if needed, and pour mixed resin into the molds. After the resin is cured, release the pieces by flexing the mold and pushing on the resin pieces from the back of the mold. If the pieces are difficult to remove, make sure the resin is completely cured. If you are sure the resin is cured, it may help to place the mold in the refrigerator or freezer for a few minutes. The cold often contracts the resin enough so that it pops out of the mold on the second attempt.

This pendant was cast using a mold made especially for resin. See fabric pendant instructions on page 54.

Bakelite-Style Bracelet

AN EARLY PLASTIC, Bakelite was a popular material used to make not only jewelry, but other household objects such as radios and toothbrushes. Brightly colored carved Bakelite bangles, pins, and other jewelry items reflect the style of the times, with Art Deco, animal, and fruit motifs. Bakelite jewelry is cheerful to wear and is highly collectible today. You can make your own retro-style "Bakelite" jewelry pieces using candy molds.

To make one bracelet, you will need:

Alumilite Regular polyurethane casting resin

Alumilite colored dyes or tints

Heart-shaped molds (Deep Flex™ molds #08-0410)

Two packages large black jump rings (Ringz by Junkitz™)

Lobster claw clasp

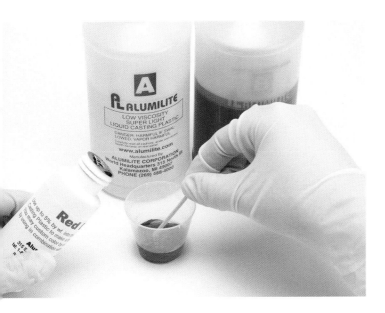

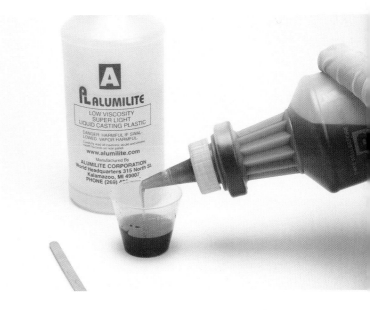

1. Make sure the molds are ready to use and placed on a flat surface. Pour ½ ounce of part A of the resin into a cup. Add a drop of red dye and stir well until color is distributed evenly.

2. Stir in ½ ounce of part B and mix well for 25 to 30 seconds. Do not whip as you stir, as this will cause more air bubbles to form.

3. Pour the resin quickly into the heart molds, filling each about ¼ inch deep. The resin will turn from transparent to opaque as it begins to set up.

After a few minutes when the resin has cured, remove the hearts from the molds by pushing on the back of the molds; they should pop out easily.

4. When the pieces are fully cured (very solid), remove any excess resin from the edges of the hearts with 100-grit sandpaper or a nail file. Refine the edges by sanding under water with finer grits of papers.

5. Drill holes in the tops of the hearts with a hand drill or pin vise.

Use pliers to open jump rings and link them together to make a chain for the bracelet. Attach a lobster claw clasp on one end. Use jump rings to attach the hearts to the chain to finish.

HEART BROOCH

You can easily make a Bakelite-style brooch to coordinate with your bracelet.

Pour the small heart and the bar shape, following the directions for the bracelet.

To make the large heart, combine 10 cc of part A of the resin with 10 cc of part B and mix well for 25 to 30 seconds. (Note: The natural color of this type of resin is ivory, so there is no need to add a colorant.)

Pour the resin quickly into the heart mold, filling about 1/4 inch deep. When the resin has cured, remove the heart from the mold.

When the pieces are fully cured (very solid), drill a hole in the top of the heart and in the center of the red bar shape with a hand drill or pin vise. At this stage you can refine the edges with sandpaper. Use epoxy adhesive to glue the small red heart to the center of the white heart.

Use jump rings to link the large heart to the bar. Glue a pin back finding to the back of the bar with epoxy adhesive.

To make one brooch, you will need:

Alumilite Regular polyurethane casting resin

Alumilite colored dyes or tints

Heart-shaped molds (Deep Flex: #08-0410 and #08-0850 G)

Bar-shaped mold (Deep Flex: #08-0409 I/Assorted Jewels)

Three large red jump rings (Ringz by Junkitz™)

Pin back finding

Devcon 2-Ton epoxy adhesive

SCATTER PINS

Rubber candy molds can be used to make whimsical retro-style scatter pins. Any small, simple shape will work.

Mix resin as directed for the bracelet or brooch if using Alumilite resin. If using Smooth-Cast 325, the process is very similar except colorant is added to Part B for this product (this is the opposite of Alumilite). Mix small batches of different colors.

Pour the resin into the molds; the resin should set up within minutes. Remove the pieces when they are cured by flexing the rubber molds. Sand the edges if needed.

You can decorate the pieces by attaching jewels or beads with epoxy adhesive. Glue pin backs to the back of each pin with epoxy adhesive.

To make several pins, you will need:

Alumilite Regular or Smooth-Cast™ 325 polyurethane casting resin

Alumilite colored dyes or tints

Rubber candy molds (Guttman Co.)

Faceted crystals, pearls, and small seed beads

Acrylic paint (optional)

Pin back findings

Devcon 2-Ton epoxy adhesive

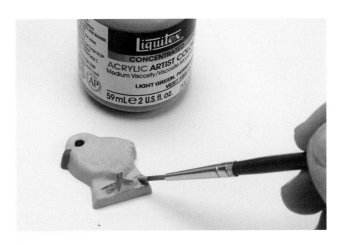

You can use acrylic paint to add details. The paint will adhere to the resin better if painted right after it is removed from the mold, before it has fully cured. Use an acrylic spray to protect the surface if desired.

Fabric Pendant

CLEAR RESIN MAGNIFIES DETAILS, bringing out the wonderful textures in fabric. You can embed any type of fabric, lace, or ribbon in resin. Some fabrics will darken as the resin soaks into the fabric. It helps to seal the fabric with decoupage glue. For this project I used fabric paper, which is treated with a coating so its color stays true and bright in the resin. I strung the pendants with crocheted cords to complement the fabric textures captured in the resin.

To make several pendants, you will need:

EasyCast clear casting epoxy

Castin'Craft opaque pigment (white)

Resin molds (Deep Flex: #08-0647 P/Teardrops)

Cotton fabric paper (Michael Miller Memories)

Craft thread (DMC®)

Small piece of craft wire for stringing beads

Assorted beads

Small metal crochet hook

Clasp (optional)

1. Make a paper pattern and cut out small shapes of fabric to fit inside the molds. Err on the side of cutting them a little smaller than the mold, so that the fabric lies flat on the resin surface rather than bending and creating air pockets in the resin.

2. Mix ½ ounce of resin to coat the bottoms of the molds and pour into the molds, filling about one-quarter full.

Place the cut fabric shapes, right side down, in the resin. Use a toothpick to press the fabric into position and to remove any air bubbles trapped under the fabric. Let the pieces cure in a warm place for several hours or overnight.

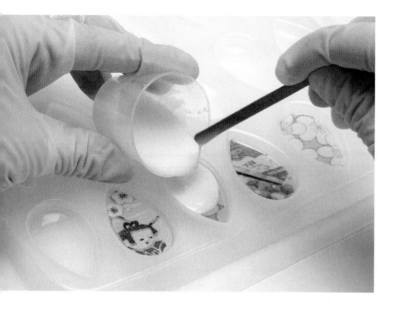

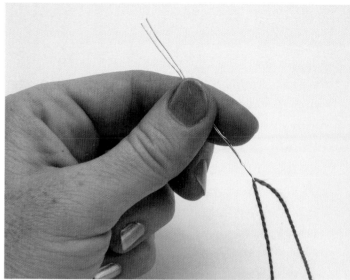

3. Mix up ½ ounce of resin and add colorant to it. Cover the fabric layers with resin.

When the pieces are cured and not tacky, remove them from the molds. Sand the edges of the pieces and drill a hole through the top of each piece with a hand drill.

4. To add a crocheted beaded cord, bend a short piece of wire over the end of the craft thread to make a "beading needle." Slide about twenty beads over the wire to add to the thread.

5. Use a small crochet hook to make a simple chain stitch. Add the beads as you go, crocheting behind each bead added. Add a bead about every five to ten stitches, as desired. Work until the chain is half of the desired finished length.

6. Fold the working end of the thread into a loop and pass it through the pendant piece. Pull both ends of the thread (beads, hook, and all) through the loop to make a lark's-head knot. Continue to crochet with beads to complete the necklace. Finish with a slipstitch. Add a clasp or simply tie to fasten the necklace.

FABRIC RINGS

You can use the same technique to make rings with embedded fabric. Small, geometric molds work best for casting shapes for rings. Follow steps 1 through 3 for making fabric pendants, but don't drill holes through the resin shapes. After the pieces are fully cured, attach ring blanks to the back of the rings using epoxy adhesive.

To make several rings, you will need:

EasyCast clear casting epoxy

Castin'Craft opaque pigment (white)

Resin molds (Deep Flex: #08-0405 I/Assorted Jewels)

Cotton fabric paper (Michael Miller Memories)

Ring blanks (Eastern Findings)

Devcon 2-Ton epoxy adhesive

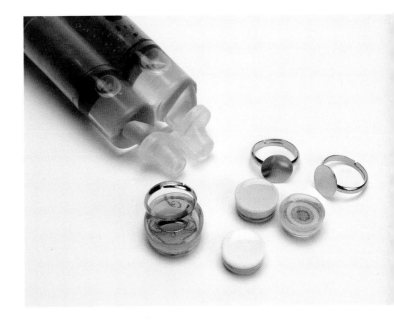

STRETCH BRACELET

To create a fabric bracelet, make resin shapes in trapezoid molds following steps 1 through 3 of the fabric pendant. Use a hand drill to drill two holes through each bead for stringing. Alternate the shapes, turning every other one the opposite direction so that the pieces fit together along the bracelet.

String the pieces along two strands of elastic cord. Tie the ends of the cord with a square knot. Use a drop of glue to seal the knots.

To make one stretch bracelet, you will need:

Cotton fabric paper (Michael Miller Memories)

EasyCast clear casting epoxy

Castin'Craft opaque pigment (white)

Resin molds (Deep Flex: #08-0405 I/ Assorted Jewels)

Elastic cord

Fabric hem sealant (Fray Check™)

Silver & Gold Leaf Jewelry

Silver or gold leaf adds a reflective mirror backing that glows through translucent resin. The leaf is applied to the back of a finished resin casting using traditional gilding methods. A layer of resin will protect the leaf from scratching off with wear. Try adding silver to cool colors and gold to warm colors of resin. Clear resin is also very pretty when backed with metal leaf.

To make one bracelet, you will need:

EasyCast clear casting epoxy

Castin'Craft transparent dyes (blue and green)

Rubber candy mold or flexible ice-cube tray

Mold release spray (ETI)

Imitation silver or gold metal leaf (composition leaf)

Leaf size (adhesive for adhering leaf)

Soft brush

Base metal bracelet findings (Eastern Findings: #7185)

Devcon 2-Ton epoxy adhesive

24-gauge silver craft wire

Purchased two-strand chain with clasp

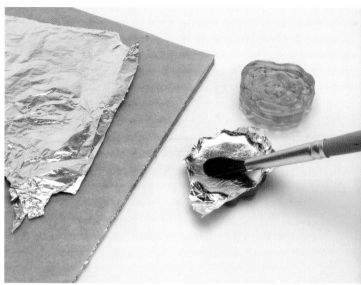

1. Mix about ½ to 1 ounce resin. Add a drop of dye to tint. You want the resin to retain as much transparency as possible to allow the leaf to shine through. Spray the molds with release spray and pour the resin into the molds. Let the resin cure overnight or until solid.

Remove the pieces and brush on a thin layer of leaf size to the back (smooth side) of each piece. Let the size dry until it turns transparent and becomes tacky (about 15 to 20 minutes).

2. Apply the leaf to the leaf size, using a soft brush to smooth. Use bits of leaf to cover any missing areas until the entire surface is covered.

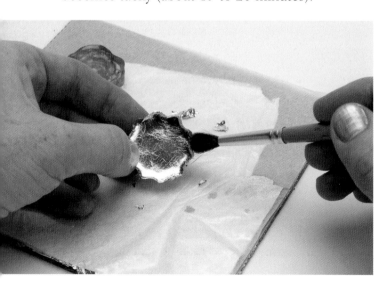

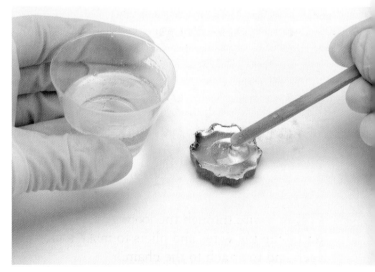

3. Use the brush to remove any excess leaf.

4. Mix a small amount of resin and apply a thin layer to cover the leaf to seal and let cure.

5. Remove the bezel pads from the bracelet findings. Bend the connector loops up with pliers.

6. Use epoxy to glue each bezel to the back of each resin piece with the loops bent away from the epoxy. Let the pieces sit until cured.

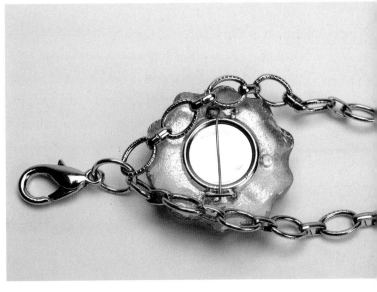

7. Run a wire through the loops. Use a wire cutter to clip the wires and pliers to make a loop at each end to attach to the chain.

8. Attach the pieces along the chains as shown, bending the wire over the chain to secure.

NECKLACE

To make a necklace, follow steps 1 through 4 for the silver-backed bracelet above, except use an amber red dye and gold leaf instead. This necklace uses only one cast piece. Drill a hole in the top of the resin piece for hanging.

Attach the resin piece to a finished necklace using a jump ring. Attach coordinating beads along the chain with jump rings to finish.

LEAF PIN

To make a pin, follow steps 1 through 4 for the silver-backed bracelet above, except use a muted purple dye to tint the resin and gold leaf to gild the resin. Attach a pin back to the back of the piece with epoxy resin adhesive.

Retro Stretch Bracelet

YOU CAN FIND GREAT RETRO IMAGES from a variety of sources to use for these theme bracelets. Clip art from books or CDs is readily available through art and scrapbook suppliers. Try using your own photos and ephemera by duplicating the images with a color copier. Black-and-white photos, a stamp collection, or clippings from an old book are a few ideas to inspire you to make a personalized bracelet.

To make one bracelet, you will need:

EasyCast clear casting epoxy

Castin'Craft opaque dyes (black or opaque red)

Resin molds (Deep Flex: Assorted Jewels #08-0407 or Rectangles #08-0412)

Photocopied images or clip art (Larger images are from the Vintage Workshop®: IE178/Shoe Bazaar, IE180/Millinery.)

Decoupage glue (Mod Podge)

Elastic cord

Fabric hem sealant (Fray Check) or superglue

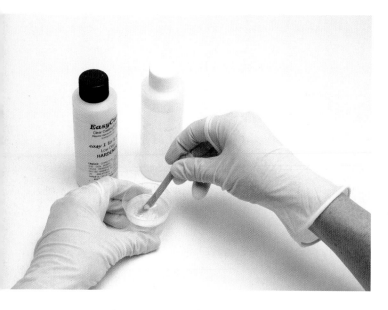

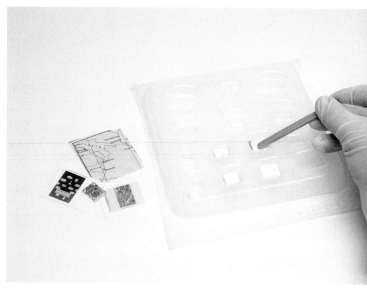

1. Cut the images to fit the molds and coat both sides plus the edges with decoupage glue to seal. Let the glue dry.

Mix equal parts resin and hardener, about ½ ounce or enough to coat the bottoms of several mold cavities.

2. Fill several cavities in the molds about one-quarter to one-third full with resin. Place the prepared images face down onto the clear resin. It helps to let the resin begin to thicken a bit before placing the images, so you can take your time placing them. Push on the images with a stir stick to remove any air trapped underneath.

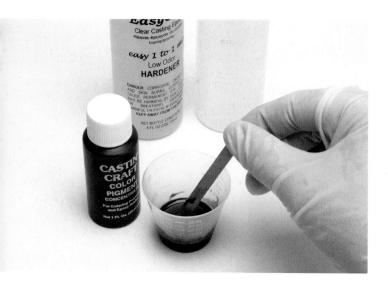

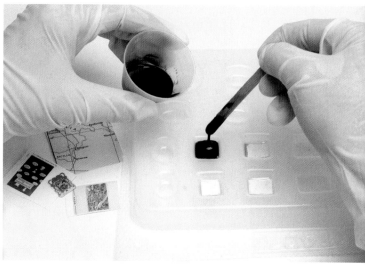

3. Let the pieces continue to cure until firm. Mix up a small amount of resin for the back of the pieces (about ½ ounce). Add a few drops of dye to the resin for color.

4. Add the resin to the back of each image in the mold, filling the mold cavities to the top with the resin.

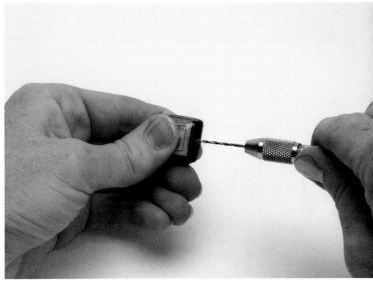

5. Use a heat gun to remove any bubbles from the resin. Let the pieces continue to cure in a warm place until hard and no longer tacky to the touch (overnight to several days).

6. When the pieces are fully cured, remove them from the mold by flexing and pushing on the back of the mold until the pieces pop out. Drill a hole through each piece with a hand drill or drill press. Drilling two holes through each piece so you can string them on two cords will help keep the beads facing the same direction around the bracelet. Clean out the shavings to clear the hole.

7. Thread the pieces onto elastic thread. Tie the ends with a square knot and seal the knot with glue.

Layered Elements Jewelry

WORKING IN LAYERS ALLOWS you to embed small objects and other inclusions to create dimension within a piece. If you are layering resin in a mold, the first layer poured is the front of the piece. The last layer poured will be the back of the piece. If you are layering into a form or bezel, the layers would be poured in the reverse order with the background being poured first.

To make one bracelet, you will need:

EasyCast clear casting epoxy

Castin'Craft opaque pigment

Mold release spray (ETI)

Resin molds (Deep Flex: #08-0410/Heart Molds)

Photocopied or clip art images

Acrylic spray (Krylon) or decoupage glue (Mod Podge)

Sequins, glitter, and other small inclusions

22- or 24-gauge craft wire

Purchased bracelet chain

Pearls or beads to embellish

Devcon 2-Ton epoxy adhesive

Project by Wendy Wallin Malinow.

1. Spray the molds with mold release spray. Let the spray dry, then repeat. Coat the paper images with decoupage glue or acrylic spray to seal the ink. Mix about ½ ounce of resin and pour a thin layer into the molds. Sprinkle glitter or a few sequins into the layer while it's still liquid. Let this layer sit until firm.

2. If you don't wish to add images, skip to step 3. Otherwise, mix about ½ ounce of clear resin for the second layer. Add this layer to the first resin layer in the molds. Place the images face down into the layer of resin. Brush resin onto the front of the image to prevent air bubbles. Let this layer cure until firm.

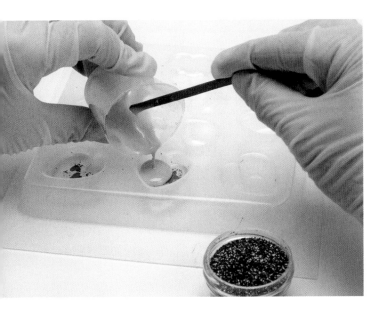

3. Mix about ½ ounce of resin for the final layer. Add a few drops of pigment and mix well. Pour into molds.

4. Sprinkle in more glitter if desired. Let the resin fully cure overnight or for several days in a warm place. Flex the mold and push from the back to release the pieces. Sand the edges.

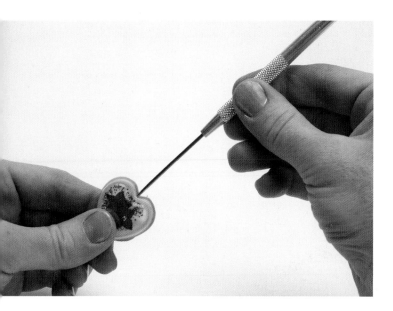

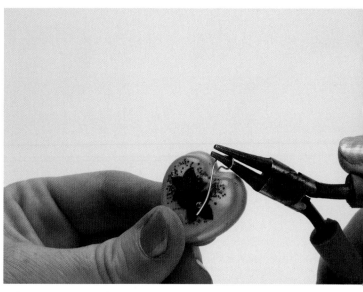

5. Use a drill to make a small hole about ¼ inch deep into the top of each heart. Clean the shavings from the hole with a needle tool.

6. Use epoxy adhesive to embed a wire into the drilled hole. Let the glue dry. Make a loop using round-nose pliers.

7. Add the finished hearts to a chain. Twist the wire around the base of the loop to secure to the chain. Clip off the excess wire.

ADDING 3-D ELEMENTS

You can also add small three-dimensional objects into the resin layers. Add the items while the resin is still liquid. To avoid air bubbles, brush a coat of resin onto the items before you add them to the liquid resin. The necklace and earrings in the photo at right were created by adding glitter to an initial layer of resin, followed by more layers of resin to which larger elements and miniature figures were added. Holes were drilled after the resin was cured to allow wire loops to be glued into place for hanging.

Glitter Gem Bead Necklace

ADD SPARKLE TO RESIN BEADS by embedding brightly colored glitter or small shimmering inclusions in the resin. Take advantage of the wide variety of glitters, micas, or small beads available on the market. Fine glitters or inclusions will suspend in the resin, whereas heavier ones, such as chunky glass glitter, tend to sink into the resin giving you multiple layers of color and texture within the bead. For best results, work with lightly tinted shades of resin so that it will remain transparent enough for the inclusions to shine through.

To make one necklace, you will need:

EasyCast clear casting epoxy

Castin'Craft transparent dye

Resin molds (Deep Flex: #08-0407 I/Assorted Jewels)

Glitter

Metal leaf

Iridescent flakes (Shaved Ice by Magic Scraps™)

Art Glitter glass shards

Small beads

24-gauge silver or gold wire craft wire

Silver or gold base metal chain

Clasp (optional)

1. To make a small batch of beads, mix 1 ounce of resin. Divide the resin into several cups and add a small amount of dye to each cup to make a variety of colors. Mix thoroughly.

2. Stir glitter, metal leaf, or iridescent flakes into the resin. Fine glitter and lighter inclusions will suspend evenly in the resin. Heavy inclusions, such as glass shards or small beads, will sink to the bottom; add these in the next step.

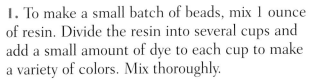

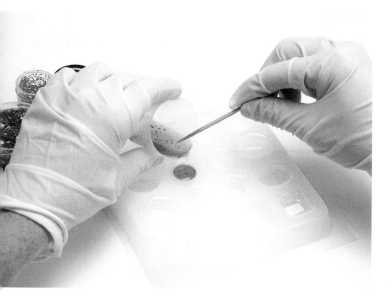

3. Pour the resin into the mold cavities. Use a heat gun to remove the air bubbles. Sprinkle heavier inclusions into the resin when it has thickened; it may take 30 minutes or longer.

Let the resin sit, undisturbed, in a warm place for 24 to 72 hours or until fully cured. Remove the pieces.

4. Use a small drill bit and a hand drill to drill a hole vertically through the center of the gem. If you have a drill press it makes the process of drilling quick and easy. To drill accurately, sometimes it helps to drill halfway through the bead and then turn it over and drill through the other direction until the holes meet in the middle. You may need to drill through the bead several times until the hole is clear of shavings.

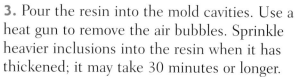

5. Sand the beads to remove raised edges. Sand under water using progressively finer grits of sandpaper.

6. Cut lengths of chain about 1 inch long each, for the space between each bead. To link the beads to the chain pieces, cut off a length of wire and thread through a bead. Form a loop in the wire at one end and thread a piece of chain onto the loop.

7. Wrap the wire at the base of the loop close to the bead and clip off the excess wire.

8. Repeat the same process on the other end of the bead to attach another length of chain. Continue adding gems and lengths of chain until the necklace is the desired length. (Finish with a longer piece of chain to fit around the back of your neck; you don't necessarily need resin beads for the back of the necklace.) If you make a long enough chain, you will not need a clasp. Add a purchased clasp for a shorter design.

Candy Jewelry

CANDY MAKES A FUN and colorful inclusion for resin. The best types of candies to embed in resin are hard candies (sour balls or suckers), gummy shapes, or sugar wafer candies (conversation hearts or Smarties). Avoid cream or chocolate candies and candies that contain moisture or a lot of oil. Candy coated with food dye will "bleed" into the resin, so this is another type to avoid. To prevent oil flavorings from leaching into the resin, treat the candy with acrylic spray before embedding.

To make one striped licorice bracelet, you will need:

EasyCast clear casting epoxy

Square molds (Castin'Craft knob and pull molds)

Mold release spray (ETI)

Striped licorice candies (sliced about ⅛ inch thick)

Acrylic spray (Krylon)

Artist's pastels

Glitter

Beads

Elastic cord

Fabric hem sealant (Fray Check) or superglue

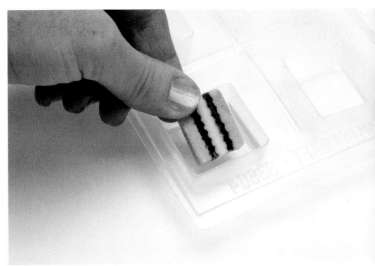

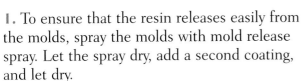

1. To ensure that the resin releases easily from the molds, spray the molds with mold release spray. Let the spray dry, add a second coating, and let dry.

Prepare the candies by slicing them if needed and spray with a coating of acrylic spray to seal. Let them dry thoroughly.

2. Mix up a small amount (about 1 ounce) of clear resin. This resin mixes in a 1:1 ratio, making it easy to measure. Mix thoroughly.

Pour a small amount in six cells of the molds, filling just the bottom (about one-quarter full) to make the first layer. Let the resin sit until it begins to thicken. Set the prepared candy slices on top of the resin. Let the pieces cure several hours or overnight in a warm place.

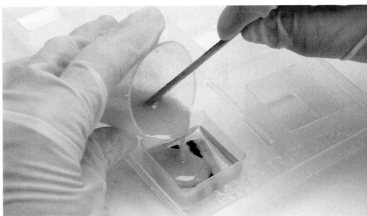

3. To add colored resin to the pieces, mix up a small batch (about 2 ounces) and divide into separate cups to mix different colors.

Use a craft knife to "shave" the pastels into the resin. It takes only a small amount to color the resin. Make sure you wear a dust mask. Mix the powdered pastels into the resin. Add glitter if desired.

4. Pour the prepared resin over the first layer of resin with the candies embedded. Let the resin cure overnight or for several days in a warm place.

As soon as the resin is cured, turn the molds over and gently press the back of the molds to release the finished pieces.

5. Drill two holes through each resin piece to string, using a hand drill or a slow-speed drill press. It helps to use a vise or clamp to hold the piece as you drill. Drill the holes through the sides, drilling from one side and then the other if necessary until the holes go all the way through the length of the piece.

6. Use a nail file (100 to 180 grit) to smooth the edges. Follow with progressively finer grits of wet/dry sandpaper if you want a nice finish.

Use elastic cord to string the pieces and beads into a bracelet. Tie the ends with a square knot. Trim and coat with hem sealant or superglue to secure the knots.

PENNY CANDY RINGS

These playful candy rings will remind you of the necklaces made of candy strung on elastic that were as much fun to wear as they were to eat. These rings are a favorite project for teens who love to wear funky accessories.

Follow steps 1 through 4 of the licorice bracelet. The candies are ready to use as is and do not need to be sealed. Pour the resin into the smaller shapes in the mold, such as the square or small circles. You can add glitter, paper, or fabric pieces to the second layer of resin for variety.

After the pieces have cured, use epoxy adhesive to attach them to ring blanks.

To make several rings, you will need:

EasyCast clear casting epoxy

Resin molds (Deep Flex: #08-0405 I or #08-0407 I /Assorted Jewels)

Mold release spray (ETI)

Smarties candies

Adjustable ring blanks (Eastern Findings)

Devcon 2-Ton epoxy adhesive

HEART PENDANTS

To make a heart pendant, follow steps 1 through 4 of the striped licorice bracelet. The heart candies do not need to be sealed; they are ready to use as is.

Use a hand drill to make a hole about ¼ inch deep in the top of the heart. Form a loop with the plastic wire, making a ¼-inch stem, and wrap the wire a few times around the stem. Glue the wire loop in place with epoxy. Hang the heart from a chain or cord.

To make several pendants, you will need:

EasyCast clear casting epoxy

Resin molds (Deep Flex: #08-0410 I/Heart Molds)

Mold release spray (ETI)

Conversation hearts candies

Artist's pastels

Glitter

Plastic-coated craft wire

Devcon 2-Ton epoxy adhesive

Chain for hanging pendant

Making Your Own
Molds for Casting

MOLDMAKING MATERIALS & TECHNIQUES

Several moldmaking products are available for creating your own custom molds for casting resin. Making your own molds gives you the freedom to cast all kinds of dimensional objects. Brass stampings, beads, buttons, doll faces, old plastic toys, and ornamental details from antiques all make great models for casting resin. You can also make molds of your own original sculptures or carvings made of polymer clay or other art materials.

Rubber molds pick up every minute detail. Perfectly smooth objects will reflect a glass-like surface on the cured resin, whereas other textures will produce a matte finish or sandblasted look. You can use the surface texture to your advantage to mimic the original material used.

To make a rubber mold, first make sure the model you choose will be suitable for casting. If it has deep undercuts or open spaces, it will be difficult or even impossible to remove from the mold. The orientation of the model will also affect how the molding material flows or is molded around it. If a model is positioned in such a way that molding material is able to work its way under and around details or "undercuts" on the model, it could become trapped in the mold, making it difficult to remove or creating air bubbles. Start with simple shapes with less detail to ensure success as you gain experience with casting and molding.

Take care when making the mold to follow all of the manufacturer's guidelines and use release agents if specified. When properly cared for, rubber molds can be used over and over again to create multiple resin castings.

Liquid moldmaking products should be handled with the same safety precautions outlined for resin on page 19. Protect your airways, eyes, and skin by wearing the appropriate protective gear.

Silicone rubber is poured through the bottom of the container.

The model is pulled from the rubber mold.

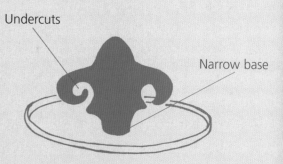

Undercuts

Narrow base

A model shaped like this example would be difficult to cast.

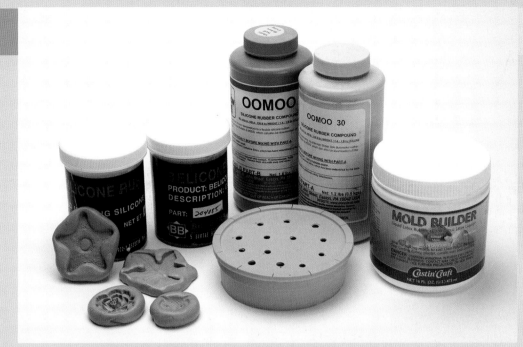

Moldmaking products from left to right: Silicone putty, liquid silicone rubber, and liquid latex rubber.

TYPES OF MOLDMAKING MATERIALS

There are several types of moldmaking products available for creating your own custom molds for casting resin.

Liquid latex consists of natural latex mixed with water and ammonia. It is brushed in layers over a model to produce a "skin"-type mold. A few of the advantages of using liquid latex is that it is inexpensive, flexible (allowing detailed shapes or undercuts to be molded), and air bubbles are minimal. The disadvantage is that it takes more time to create the mold than a pour-type rubber. You have to brush on many layers over the model, letting each dry before adding the next. Because this is a water-based material, make sure it is thoroughly dry before casting, especially if using polyurethane resins.

Liquid silicone rubber molds are popular for casting figurines. Also referred to as room-temperature-vulcanizing (RTV) silicone rubber molds, there are many brands available through modelmaking suppliers. The product is packaged as a two-part system of silicone plus a curative. To make a mold, the two parts are mixed together thoroughly at room temperature, then poured over a model in a contained area and left to cure.

There are a few things to consider when choosing a silicone rubber material for your project. Formulations based on equal ratios (1 part A + 1 part B) are the easiest to use as they do not require a scale to mix. Another factor to keep in mind is that some types must be processed or placed in a vacuum to remove air bubbles. The silicone rubber products used in this book do not require a scale or vacuum.

The nice thing about this type of moldmaking material is that it does not usually require a release agent. The cured silicone mold is flexible and can be pulled or stretched away from the original model. In turn, resin castings are removed from the mold as easily as the original model was.

A warm environment is necessary for proper curing. Let the poured mold cure undisturbed in a warm place. To facilitate curing, you can place the mold under a lamp or low-watt bulb to keep it warm. For example, it should take about 1½ to 2 hours for OOMOO™ 25 to become firm enough to remove the model. After the model is removed, it's a good idea to let the rubber sit and continue to cure. Even if the rubber is firm, moisture and vapors will continue to be emitted from the rubber as it cures. If resin is poured into the mold soon after removing the model, the vapors may cause air bubbles to form in the resin as they escape from the mold.

Polyurethane rubber molds are similar to silicone rubbers in that they come in a two-part system and produce flexible finished molds. The molds are very durable, allowing for multiple castings. Other advantages are that it is available in a wide range of hardnesses, it traps less air (therefore not requiring a vacuum), and is less expensive than silicone.

The disadvantage is that the polyurethane adheres tightly to most surfaces, requiring a release agent for both the model and the cast resin pieces. Because this type of material is more involved in terms of mold preparation and safety concerns, it has not been used for the projects in this book. However, it is a favorite material for those who cast production work and should not be discounted if you have a shop or facility with proper safety equipment and ventilation.

Silicone putty mold compounds are probably the easiest of all to use. The fun thing about this material is that you can take it with you to make molds on location. Try capturing items from nature or the ornamental relief of architectural details you might find in your travels. See steps for working with silicone putty at right.

DETERMINING VOLUME FOR MOLDS

Before mixing a moldmaking product, it's worth taking the time to figure out how much you will need, since the material is expensive to waste. You can calculate volume using a mathematical formula for the cubic area of the mold. A simpler method is to fill the container that will hold the mold with water. Pour the water into a measuring cup and note the amount needed. Make sure you dry the inside of the mold thoroughly before use. You can round the amount down as your original model will occupy space in the mold, decreasing the amount needed.

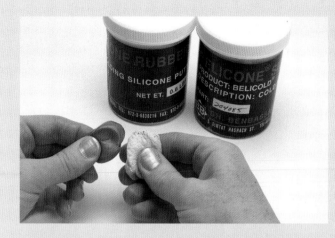

1. Silicone putty is sold in two parts, with each component being a separate color.

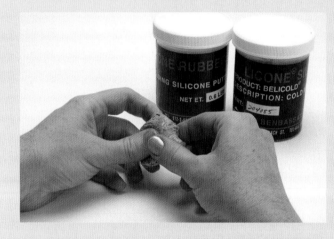

2. Simply knead the components (A + B) with your hands until thoroughly blended (colors combine to make one solid color).

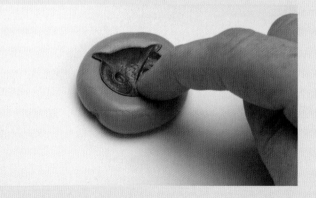

3. You can either press the model into the putty or press the putty over the object. The putty cures in minutes, or even faster at warm temperatures. Remove the model from the cured putty.

Faux Celluloid Bracelet

CELLULOID WAS ONE OF THE EARLIEST forms of modern day plastic. It is a semisynthetic material that was used to imitate ivory, tortoiseshell, and horn. Carved celluloid jewelry was popular in the 1920s and '30s. Beautifully detailed carved buttons, pins, and bangles can be purchased from antique shops or through auction sites online. Pigments and dyes can be added to resin to allow you to replicate antique celluloid in vintage shades of ivory, coral, tortoiseshell, or black, to name just a few.

To make one bracelet, you will need:

Carved celluloid bracelet or plastic replica to use as the model

OOMOO 25 silicone rubber

Alumilite Regular polyurethane resin (ivory)

Yogurt or plastic take-out container with lid

Wax, modeling clay, or polymer clay (Sculpey III™)

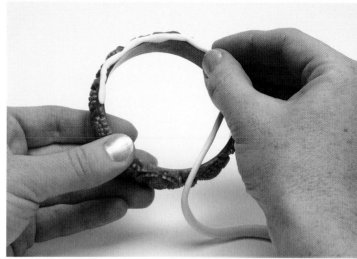

1. Start by choosing an original piece of jewelry for your model. Although celluloid pieces are usually very ornate with dimensional carvings, look for pieces that have low relief and few undercuts. This will provide you with a successful resin casting that is easier to remove from the mold and less likely to trap air bubbles that might affect the quality of the piece.

2. Remove the bottom of the plastic container. Use a strip of wax or clay to attach the bracelet (model) to the inside of the lid. Make sure there are no gaps under the bracelet where rubber might seep under and through open spaces.

To conserve silicone rubber, place a large plug of polymer clay in the center of the bracelet. Leave at least ½ inch of space on either side of the bracelet to fill with rubber.

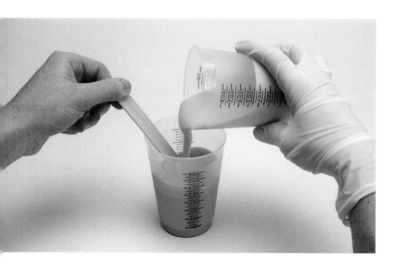

3. Replace the container, snapping it to the lid securely. Mix the silicone rubber according to the manufacturer's instructions. Stir the rubber for a full 3 minutes, scraping the sides of the container well. Do not whip the mixture as this introduces air bubbles. Stir gently but thoroughly.

4. Pour the prepared liquid into the container. Pour in the lowest area first, allowing the rubber to surround and cover the model by at least ¼ to ½ inch over the highest point. Tap the mold to release air bubbles. Let the mold cure in a warm place. It should take about 1½ to 2 hours.

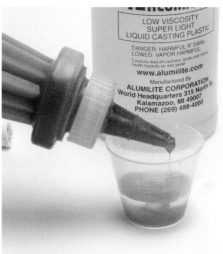
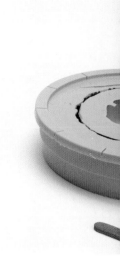

5. When the rubber is firm, remove the lid and pull the mold from the container. Remove the strip of clay. If a thin layer of rubber found its way under the model, it can be trimmed away with small scissors or a craft knife. Remove the plug of clay from the center.

Remove the model by gently prying the rubber away. After removing the original model, let the rubber continue to cure in a warm place.

6. Measure out parts A and B of the resin into separate cups (10 cc to ½ ounce each). Pour part A into part B and stir, but don't "whip." Make sure to scrape the sides of the cup thoroughly. Mix for about 15 to 25 seconds, you have only a few minutes in which to work.

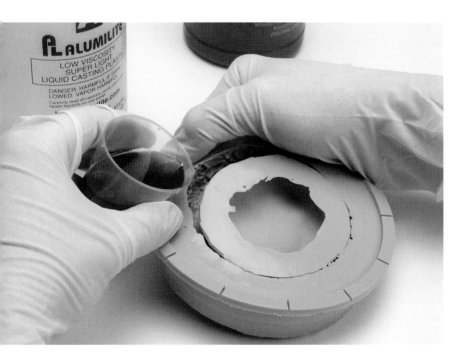

7. Pour the resin quickly into the rubber mold, coaxing the resin in by flexing the mold open. The resin will harden and change to an opaque color as it cures. Note: The resin cures better in warm temperatures; you can pre-heat the mold by placing it under a low-watt bulb prior to casting.

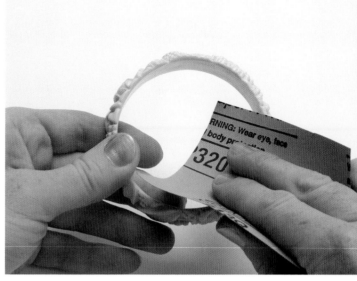

8. De-mold the resin as soon as it is firm, usually within an hour, by flexing the mold and gently prying the edges of the rubber away from the cured resin. It helps to push from the bottom of the mold as well.

9. At this stage the resin is still soft and flexible. Use this to your advantage to trim away any resin left around the bracelet. Small scissors or a craft knife work well. Use sandpapers to smooth the edges.

ROSE PENDANT AND EARRINGS

This is a good project for using up any resin left over from the bracelet project. Have the molds prepared and ready to go as the resin cures quickly.

To make the pendant, pinch off a marble-size piece of each component of putty. Knead the putty together until a uniform color is obtained.

Press the button (large for pendant or small for earrings) into the putty and let the mold cure for about 10 to 30 minutes. The button will be easy to remove. Let the mold continue to cure overnight to ensure all of the moisture has evaporated.

Prepare the resin as directed in the instructions for the celluloid bracelet.

To make one pendant or pair of earrings, you will need:

Large rose-shaped button (for the pendant)

Small rose-shaped button (for the earrings)

Belicone® silicone rubber putty

Alumilite Regular polyurethane resin (ivory)

Pour the resin into the mold. After the resin sets, remove the excess from around the edges of the cast piece with a craft knife and sand the edges. Cast two resin roses to make earrings.

Drill a hole in the top of the rose with a small drill. Make a loop out of 24-gauge wire and attach to the rose, wrapping the wire to connect. Join beads and pearls with wire to form a beaded chain for each side of the necklace. Add a clasp to finish. To make earrings, drill a hole through each rose for hanging and add ear wires with pliers; you can add a bead with wire between the rose and the hook for a dressier look.

Pod Bead Bracelet

THE "PODS" ON THIS BRACELET were created by sculpting freeform shapes in polymer clay, then using the shapes as models to make a rubber mold. The trick is to make simple shapes that will be easy to remove from the mold. Variation in hue and scale of the cast shapes gives the bracelet rhythm and movement.

To make one bracelet, you will need:

Smooth-Cast 327 polyurethane resin

Colorant for tinting resin (So-Strong™)

Plastic yogurt or take-out container with lid

OOMOO 25 liquid silicone rubber

2 ounces polymer clay (Premo™ or Sculpey III)

Plastic-coated craft or telephone wire

Devcon 2-Ton epoxy adhesive

Cord or elastic

Fabric hem sealant (Fray Check)

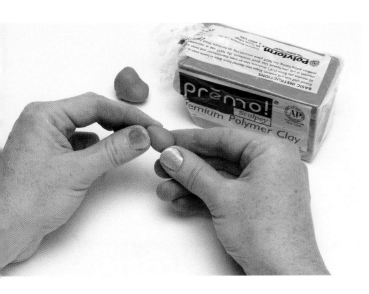

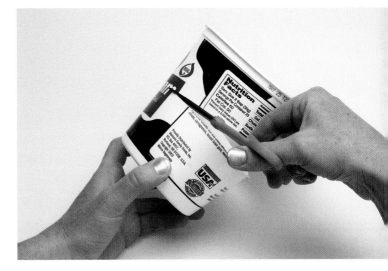

1. Knead polymer clay in your hands until soft. Make teardrop shapes in various sizes. Set them on a glass baking dish or tile, rounded side down, pointed end up; press them firmly onto the glass. Bake in a toaster oven at 275°F for 30 minutes. Let the pieces cool in the oven.

2. Remove the bottom of the plastic container, as it will be placed lid side down.

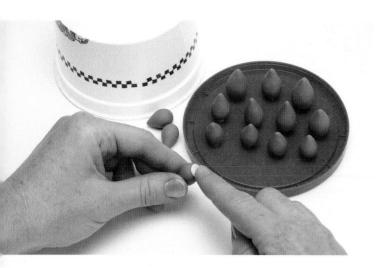

3. Use a small bit of unbaked polymer clay at the base of each polymer piece to attach them onto the inside of the plastic lid of the container. Leave room between the shapes, spacing them evenly on the lid. Leave at least ½ inch around the outer edge between the shapes and the lid.

4. Mix the silicone rubber according to the manufacturer's instructions. Stir the rubber for a full 3 minutes. Stir gently but thoroughly.

Pour the rubber into the container, letting the rubber rise to surround and cover the polymer pieces by at least ¼ to ½ inch. Tap the mold to release air bubbles. Let the mold cure in a warm place. It should take about 1½ to 2 hours.

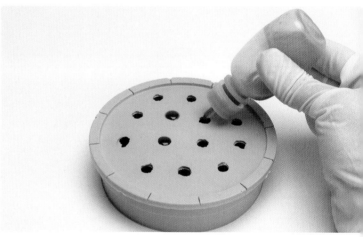

5. When the rubber is firm, remove the lid and pull the entire mold from the container. Remove the pieces of polymer clay by flexing the mold and pushing on the underside or bottom of the mold. Don't worry if a thin layer of rubber found its way under the pieces covering the unbaked clay. This can be trimmed away with small scissors or a craft knife as you remove the clay.

After removing the original pieces, let the rubber continue to cure in a warm place.

6. Measure out parts A and B of the resin into separate cups (10 cc to ½ ounce each). To tint the resin, add a tiny bit of colorant with the tip of a toothpick to part B first and stir.

Pour the resin into a small bottle to aid pouring. Fill each of the cavities in the mold until the resin reaches the top. If you overfill, you can remove the excess resin after the pieces are cured. Let the resin cure for at least 4 to 6 hours or overnight.

7. De-mold the resin pieces by flexing the mold and gently prying the edges of the rubber away from the sides of the cured resin. It helps to push from the bottom of the mold as well. The pieces should pop out easily with firm even pressure from the bottom of the mold.

Sand the excess resin from each cured piece following the instructions on page 28.

8. Make small loops with plastic-coated wire to hang the beads. Start by making a loop in the wire, leaving a small, ¼-inch stem of wire. Twist the wire around the stem a few times and clip. Make a loop for each bead.

9. Use a pin vise with a ³⁄₃₂-inch drill bit to drill about ¼ inch into the base of each bead. Glue the loops into the holes with epoxy adhesive.

To make a bracelet, start with about 18 inches of cord. Leaving about 2 inches on the end, begin tying each bead with a single knot along the cord. Space the knots about ¼ inch apart.

When you have added enough beads to fit around your wrist, tie a loop after the last bead to create a "loop and toggle" type closure. Clip off the excess cord and seal with hem sealant.

Faux Jade Neckpiece

JADE IS A GEMSTONE THAT possesses transparent and opaque qualities within the same stone. Like many other gemstones, it ranges vastly in color and texture. Green, ranging from pale light green to dark emerald, is the color most often associated with jade. By mixing various shades and opacities of green resin, you can simulate the look of jade. Pouring techniques allow you to re-create streaks or "veins" that are found in natural jade.

To make one jade neckpiece, you will need:

Purchased/found antiquity for model (antiquities courtesy of Jacqueline Lee)

OOMOO 25 liquid silicone rubber

Plastic food container with lid

Double-sided adhesive sheet (PEELnSTICK™)

EasyCast clear casting epoxy

Transparent yellow, transparent green, amber, and white dyes (Castin'Craft)

Vintage Milk Paints (Aspen Art Stamps)

Plastic-coated beading wire

Stone beads and pearls

Crimp beads

Clasp

1. Follow steps 1 through 11 on pages 97 through 100 to make a rubber mold of the piece to be used as the model for the mold. Use a double-sided adhesive sheet to attach the model to the inside of the plastid lid, making sure the lid is large enough for rubber to surround the pieces. After the mold has cured, remove the pieces.

2. Mix ½ ounce resin, stirring well. Pour half of the resin into one cup and divide the remaining resin between two other cups. Add a drop or two of transparent green, muted with a small amount of amber and yellow dye, to the cup that contains half the mixture. (Use a toothpick to control the amount.) In one of the other cups mix a little green with white to make an opaque light green. Mix amber with just a hint of green in the remaining cup. This photo shows a palette of dyes to use for the resin.

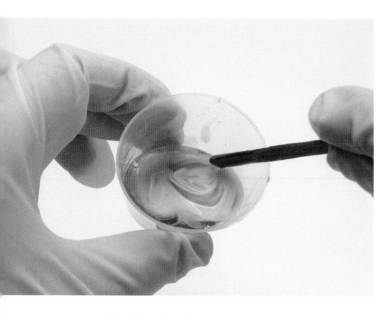

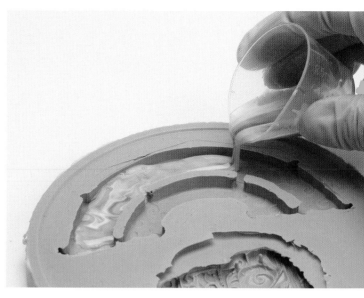

3. Gently fold the three colors together, swirling with a stick. Don't over-mix.

4. Pour the resin into the prepared mold.

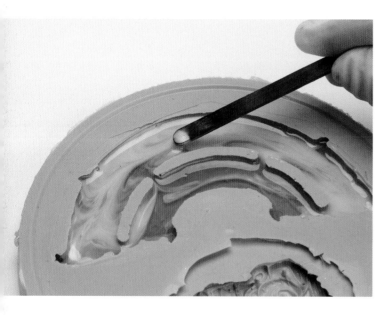

5. Create "vein" patterns by gently pulling a stick through the resin.

Let the resin cure in a warm place overnight or until firm and remove from the mold. Sand the edges on the back of the piece.

6. To antique the piece, paint with Milk Paint following manufacturer's instructions. Adding a little white glue to the paint will help the color to adhere in the recessed areas. Use a damp cloth to wipe the paint off the high spots while the paint is still wet.

7. Buff the surface with car wax to seal and protect the paint. Work in a circular motion with a soft cloth as you buff.

String the neckpiece using beading wire with beads to coordinate. Add crimp beads and a clasp to finish.

FAUX CARNELIAN

This stone is created similarly to the faux jade formula. Use transparent colors of rich reds and brown hues to create the look of carnelian. Ancient-looking beads and macramé cord help to complete the antiquity-style necklace.

The carnelian is mixed using the following resin colors: Mix ½ ounce resin, adding a drop of transparent red. Pour a small amount of this resin into two other cups. Add a bit of opaque brown to one and opaque white to the other. Swirl the colors as in step 3 for making faux jade.

Pour the resin into the prepared mold. Let the resin cure and remove from the mold.

Drill a hole in each side of the finished pendant. A macramé stitch (half-hitch knot) was used with cord to complete the necklace. Add beads into the knotting to complete the design.

Bangle Bracelets

A BANGLE BRACELET IS AN EASY shape to cast in resin. Crushed glass was added to the resin to give the appearance of sandblasted glass. The same mold created for this bangle could be used with techniques borrowed from other projects. The bangle could be cast with various resins and colorants to mimic jade, amber, or bakelite. You can add inclusions such as glitter, fabric, fibers, and images to a transparent bangle for a fascinating effect. A smooth, simple bracelet form works best as a model for this project.

To make one bangle bracelet, you will need:

Purchased bangle

OOMOO 25 silicone rubber

Double-sided adhesive sheet (PEELnSTICK)

2 ounces sulfur-free polymer clay such as Premo or Sculpey (optional)

Smooth-Cast 327 polyurethane resin

So-Strong colorant for tinting resin

Crushed glass (National Artcraft Co.)

Yogurt or plastic take-out container with lid

1. Remove the bottom of the plastic container. (The container will be placed lid side down.)

2. Apply a sheet of double-sided adhesive to one side of the bracelet (this will be used to attach the bracelet to the inside of the lid).

3. Trim off the excess around the bracelet.

4. Attach the bracelet to the inside of the lid. Make sure there are no gaps under the bracelet where rubber might seep through. Optional: Add a lump of polymer clay to the middle to displace and save the amount of rubber needed for the mold. (Note: Sulfur-free clays will not react with the resin.)

5. Replace the container, snapping it to the lid securely.

6. Measure about 4 ounces each of part A and part B, depending on the size of the container you are using for the mold.

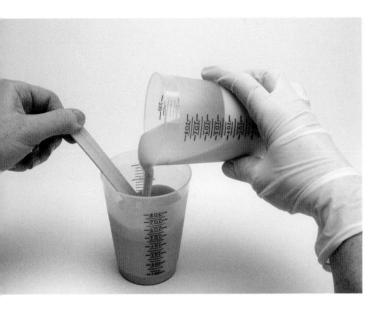

7. Mix parts A and B together and stir the rubber for a full 3 minutes, scraping the sides of the container well. Do not whip the mixture as this will introduce air bubbles.

8. Stir gently but thoroughly.

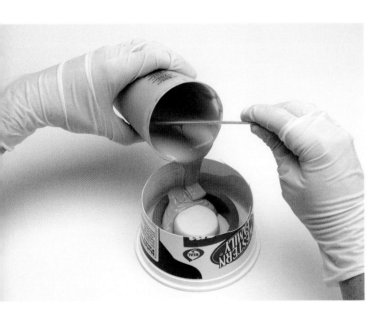

9. Pour the prepared liquid into the container, pouring in the lowest area first. Let the rubber rise to surround and cover the model.

10. Cover the model by at least ¼ to ½ inch over the highest point. Tap the mold to release air bubbles (as you would with cake batter). Let the mold cure in a warm place until firm. To facilitate curing, you can place the mold under a low-watt bulb to keep it warm. It should take about 1½ to 2 hours for OOMOO 25.

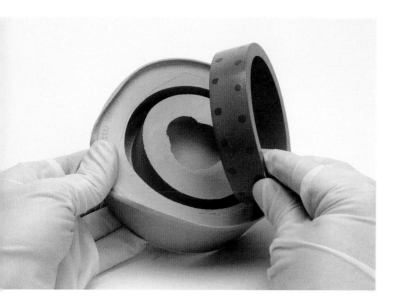

11. When the rubber is firm, remove the lid and pull the mold from the container. Remove the tape from the base of the bracelet. Don't worry if rubber found its way under the model. It can be trimmed away with scissors or a craft knife.

Remove the model by prying the rubber away and flexing the mold. After removing the model, let the rubber continue to cure in a warm place.

12. To prepare the resin, measure out ½ ounce each of parts A and B into separate cups. If you want to tint the resin, add a tiny bit of coloring with the tip of a toothpick to part B first and stir.

Mix the resin and pour it quickly into the rubber mold. Pour a little resin first, then crushed glass, filling almost to the top.

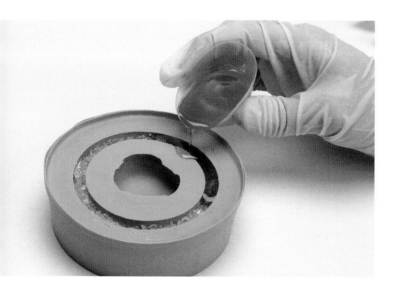

13. Fill with the remaining resin until the resin reaches the top of the mold. The resin will harden as it cures. This should take 4 to 6 hours, or leave overnight. Note: The resin cures better in warm temperatures; you can pre-heat the mold by placing it under a lamp or low-watt bulb prior to casting.

14. When the resin is cured, remove it by flexing the mold and gently prying the edges of the rubber away from the sides of the cured resin. It helps to push from the bottom of the mold as well.

Use wet/dry sandpapers under water to smooth the rough edges.

Faux Amber Jewelry

AMBER IS FOSSILIZED RESIN formed from ancient trees similar to pines or spruce trees. Organic matter (plants and insects) trapped in the resin is part of the beauty and value of natural amber. Although amber is most often thought of as a warm honey color, it's actually available in many colors. The most common colors range from light butter yellow to dark brown. Other colors include cherry amber with reddish-brown tones, green with lemon or olive undertones, and shades of blue. Artist Marie Browning has developed techniques for imitating many different materials. This project was inspired by her.

To make one bracelet or necklace, you will need:

Large plastic beads to mold

Belicone silicone putty

Mold for pendant (Deep Flex: #08-0406 I/Teardrop Shapes)

EasyCast clear casting epoxy

Amber and transparent yellow dyes (Castin'Craft)

Dried organic matter (bits of bark, leaves, flower petals)

Gold or bronze metal leaf

Clasp finding

Plastic-coated beading wire

Crimp beads

Silver beads (optional)

1. Prepare the molds for the nugget beads by mixing a small ball of each silicone putty compound together. Knead thoroughly until color is uniform.

Mold the putty around one large bead at a time. Leave an opening exposed at the top of the bead. Position the bead in the putty with the largest surface area at the top to make it easier to remove.

Mold additional beads and remove the beads after about 30 minutes or when the mold is cured. It's best to make the molds several days before casting the resin to allow the molds to continue to release moisture as they cure.

2. Use a purchased resin mold to make a large teardrop shape for the amber pendant.

Mix the resin following manufacturer's instructions. About ½ to 1 ounce resin will fill enough molds to make a handful of beads. Add a few drops of amber-colored dye and one or two drops of transparent yellow until you are pleased with the color. To make other shades or colors, follow the guide on page 105.

3. Prepare flakes of metal leaf by clipping the leaf with the tip of scissors. Break up small pieces of organic matter, such as bits of dried bark, leaves, or flowers. Make sure the pieces are thoroughly dried; you don't want any plant oils found in fresh plants to react with the resin.

4. Sprinkle a pinch of the metal leaf and organic bits into the resin, stirring to mix. Heavier pieces will sink to the bottom of the molds, so you may want to sprinkle the organic bits after pouring resin into the molds.

5. Pour the resin into the prepared molds.

6. Use a heat gun to remove air bubbles from the resin.

7. Let the resin cure until hardened, at least overnight or for several days. Pop the pieces out of the molds.

8. Sand the edges with wet/dry sandpapers. For extra shine, buff the surface of the resin with fine polishing cloths and car wax as a final step.

9. Drill a hole in each finished piece. Drill through the center of the beads to be used for the bracelet and necklace, and drill through the top of the pendant bead.

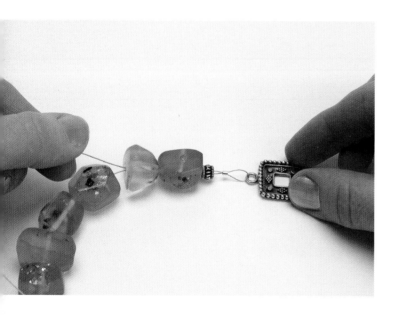

10. String the amber beads on a piece of beading wire, adding silver beads if desired to the design.

11. Finish the bracelet by adding a purchased clasp to each end and crimping the wire with crimp beads to hold. String the necklace in the same fashion, positioning the molded pendant piece in the center of the nuggets. Natural amber chips were used to finish the rest of the strand before adding a clasp.

EARRINGS

To make a pair of earrings, cast two teardrop-shaped nuggets and two small square shapes following the instructions for making the bracelet and necklace nuggets. After the resin is cured, drill a hole through each of the smaller square shapes. Add a head pin and small spacer, forming a loop at the bottom to hang the teardrop. Drill holes to glue a wire into the top of each teardrop. After the glue dries, add a bead cap over each wire. Form a loop with the wire to attach the teardrop to the square shapes. Glue earring findings to the back of the square shapes to finish.

To make one pair of earrings, you will need:

EasyCast clear casting epoxy

Transparent green, transparent yellow, and transparent amber dyes (Castin'Craft)

Resin molds (Deep Flex: #08-0406 I/Teardrop Shapes and #08-0407 I/Assorted Jewels)

Dried organic matter

Gold or bronze leaf

Two pieces of 22- or 24-gauge silver wire (about 4 inches each)

Two silver head pins

Two small silver spacer beads

Two silver filigree bead caps

Two earring post findings

Devcon 2-Ton epoxy adhesive

AMBER COLOR FORMULAS

Here are a few dye combinations you can try to make different colors of faux amber.

Golden yellow amber: A few drops amber dye, plus one or two drops transparent yellow

Dark amber: Several drops of transparent amber dye

Cherry red amber: Several drops of transparent red plus a drop each of transparent amber and dark brown

Green amber: Three drops transparent green, a drop or two of transparent yellow, and a small drop of transparent amber

Combining Resin with Polymer Clay

WORKING WITH POLYMER CLAY

Polymer clay is a colorful, pliable, oven-curing clay that is available in craft and hobby stores. It comes in many colors, including metallic gold, silver, bronze, and pearl shades. There are also translucent clays and liquid forms of polymer clay. Polymer clay is made of particles of polyvinyl chloride (PVC) with a plasticizer added to make the material flexible and pliable. There are a variety of techniques available to create all kinds of effects with the clay. The clay can be modified to imitate stone, ivory, glass, or metal. It can also be combined with paint, metal leaf, pigment powders, and other art materials.

Polymer clay is a wonderful companion product for resin. It can be combined with resin to create a mixed media piece, or it can be used as a tool for moldmaking. Like resin, polymer clay is a plastic, and the colors and textures complement each other nicely.

For decorative purposes, the clay can be used in cured (or baked) form to make bezels, backgrounds, and decorative elements for resin. Cured pieces of polymer clay also make colorful inclusions to embed in resin.

Un-baked, polymer clay is useful as a material for moldmaking. Polymer clay can act as an adhesive or prop when preparing models. The clay is easy to remove from rubber or resin, and can be reused. Premo or Sculpey brand polymer clays are used for the projects in this book when unbaked clay is called for because these brands are nonreactive with resin and silicone rubber. You can use other brands of polymer and modeling clays, but make sure they are sulfur-free or they will cause curing problems and leave sticky spots in molds.

Polymer clay must be conditioned after opening the package. To condition the clay, knead it with your hands until it is soft and pliable. Pasta machines can be used to make nice even sheets of clay in varying thicknesses. (This tool should be dedicated for use with polymer clay, as should all tools used with the clay. Polymer clay should not come into contact with any food handling items.) After conditioning the clay you can sculpt, roll, or shape the clay any way you would like.

Bake polymer clay on a glass baking dish, ceramic tile, or clean piece of paper in an oven. For those who use polymer clay frequently, it's best to use a toaster oven dedicated to polymer clay (not for food). Most polymer clay brands can be baked at 275°F for 30 minutes. Polymer clay emits toxic fumes if fired above the temperature given by the manufacturer. Let the clay cool in the oven for a stronger finished product. The particles fuse into a hardened piece. When properly fused, the clay remains strong and flexible after baking.

After baking, polymer clay can be carved, sanded, buffed, or left as is. Sanding and buffing create a smooth and shiny surface on the clay. The process is almost identical to sanding resin, although polymer clay is quite a bit softer than resin, so you should begin with 400- or maybe 320-grit sandpaper. For the projects in this book, sanding was not required.

Tools for working with polymer clay: pasta machine, clay roller, and assorted cutting and sculpting tools.

Sequined Belt Buckle

BELT BUCKLE BLANKS PROVIDE a large bezel ideal for filling with resin and other elements. Belt buckles are available through jewelry suppliers. Look for purchased belts that can be snapped into the buckle.

The polymer clay used for the background for this buckle design features a colorful clay gradient developed by artist Judith Skinner. The "Skinner blend" is a method to make a smooth gradation using two or more colors of polymer clay. The gradient is formed by repeatedly rolling the colors through a pasta maker to blend them.

To make one belt, you will need:

Magenta, orange, and pearl polymer clay (Kato Polyclay™)

Pasta machine

Waxed paper

Double-sided tape

Belt buckle blank (Jewelry Supply: #BU202)

Assorted sequins

Glitter

Beads

White glue

EasyCast clear casting epoxy

Purchased belt

Project by Jacqueline Lee.

1. Mix eight parts magenta clay with one part pearl for one color and then eight parts orange with one part pearl.

To make a Skinner blend, roll out each color of clay in the pasta roller at setting #1 (thickest). Cut rectangles of each color about 4 by 2½ inches and then cut the rectangles into triangles. Combine one triangle of each color to form a rectangle. Press the seam to join the colors.

Fold the polymer rectangle in half, bringing the short ends together so that the point of a triangle is met by its own base of the same color. Run the folded polymer clay rectangle through the pasta roller at setting #1.

2. Fold the clay (always in the same direction) and run through the pasta roller repeatedly, until a gradient forms. It may take ten times or more. Finish rolling when you are pleased with the gradient.

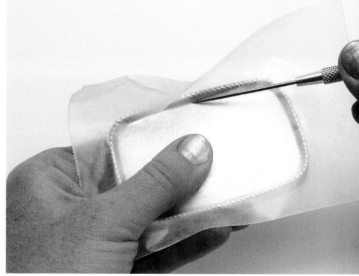

3. Make a pattern for the clay: Use double-sided tape to secure a piece of waxed paper to the center of the bezel area of the buckle and then score around the interior edge with a needle tool to make a pattern. If your belt buckle is not perfectly symmetrical, mark your pattern so that you can identify the correct orientation.

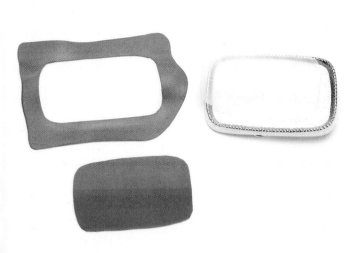

4. Lay the belt buckle pattern on the clay and cut around it with a craft knife. Place the clay in the belt buckle. Bake at 275°F degrees for 30 minutes. Cool completely in the oven.

5. Use white glue to attach assorted sequins and small beads to the baked clay surface.

6. Use small cups or something similar to prop the buckle and allow it to sit level. Mix a small batch of resin and stir well. Pour the resin into the buckle to cover the sequins and beads. Sprinkle glitter or more sequins into the resin if desired. Let the resin cure in a warm place for several days.

Project by Jacqueline Lee.

Techno Polymer Clay Bezels

COMMON ITEMS FROM the hardware store, such as small washers and galvanized cable, offer nontraditional jewelry materials to use in your work. Hardware parts combined with red and black polymer clay give these bezels a bold industrial style. The same techniques can be applied to organically shaped bezels in soft colors. Embed natural elements into the resin for an entirely different look.

To make one necklace, you will need:

Red, black, and white polymer clay (Kato Polyclay)

Kato clear liquid medium

Pasta machine

Silver leaf

Sandpaper (50 grit)

Circle cutters (Kemper)

Square cutter (optional)

Small drinking straws (for cutting holes)

Two small screw eyes (½ inch long, wire size 16)

One 10-24 coupling nut (for the bail)

Assorted washers and hex nuts

Clear casting epoxy (EasyCast)

18-inch piece of ⅟₃₂ galvanized cable

2mm hook-and-eye crimp clasp set (Rio Grande: #690636)

1. Condition the polymer clays according to the package directions. Roll out a sheet of black clay on the thickest setting of the pasta machine. Texture the clay by rolling it through the machine again with a small piece of 50-grit sandpaper.

   Cut out the modified triangle shape as shown.

2. Roll out a sheet of red clay on setting #4 (on a pasta roller for which #1 is the thickest setting) and cut out the circle shapes as shown. Roll out a sheet of black clay on setting #4. Cut out a small rectangle and lay it on a piece of silver leaf (this is easier than trying to lay the leaf on the clay). Roll the leaf-covered clay through the pasta machine again on the same setting. Cut out circle shapes as shown. Make tiny holes in the red and silver circles with small circle cutters or drinking straws.

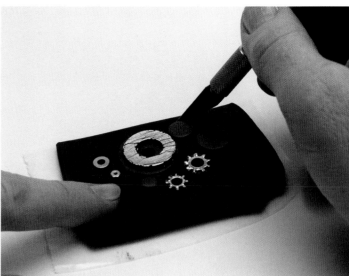

3. Arrange the elements, including the hardware, as shown. Press the metal elements lightly into the clay. Bake the clay for 20 minutes on a glass baking dish or smooth tile at 275°F and cool in the oven.

4. Lay the baked piece on a fresh sheet of black clay rolled out at the thickest setting. Cut around the baked piece. This raw lower layer will help your clay bezel stick and will provide the needed thickness for attaching the screw eyes.

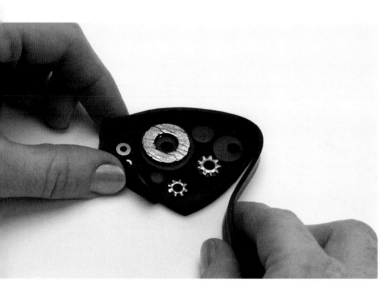

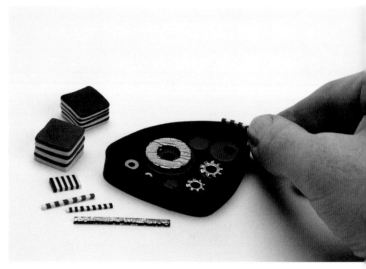

5. Roll out a sheet of black clay on setting #4 and cut a strip ½ inch wide and long enough to wrap around the decorated piece with some overlap. Wrap the clay strip around the piece. Cut the excess clay away to form a butt joint. Smooth the seams with your fingers or use a clay shaping tool or blunt needle tool for more control, especially on the inside seam.

Bake the pendant at 275°F for 20 minutes. Let cool in oven.

6. Roll sheets of white and red clay on setting #4. Cut several pieces of each color by hand or with a square cutter. Make a stack, alternating colors. Let the clay rest for at least an hour. Repeat the process with black and white clays.

When the clay has rested or cooled, cut thin slices as shown. Trim the slices to the desired length and use them to decorate, placing a *very* thin layer of Kato clear liquid medium between each element and the bezel.

7. Cut a small strip of the leafed clay and use the Kato clear liquid medium to adhere it to the top edge of the bezel. Bake the pendant a final time for 40 minutes at 275°F.

Use a needle tool to mark the placement for the screw eyes, leaving enough space for the coupling nut in between. Make certain that you place them so that they will be screwed into the double-layer base.

Screw the eyes into the pendant.

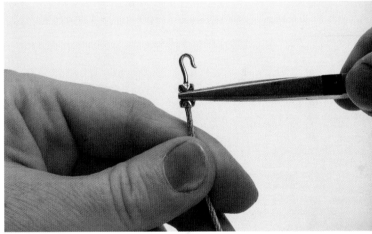

8. Place the coupling nut between the eye pins and feed the cable through the holes. The one in the photo was wrapped with a strip of black clay and pre-baked as a decorative option.

9. Crimp the clasp ends onto the cable with pliers.

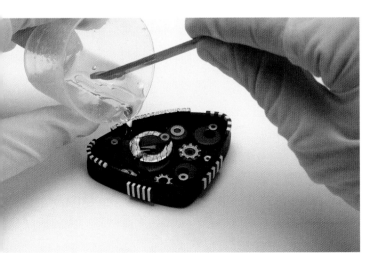

10. Set the pendant on a level surface to add the resin. Mix a small amount of resin (about ½ ounce) to pour into the bezel. Pour starting in the lowest area until the resin is level with the top of the bezel. Use a heat gun to remove the bubbles. Let it sit undisturbed in a warm place overnight, or for several days, until cured.

Project by Wendy Wallin Malinow.

Funky Flower Pins

THESE PINS ARE REPRESENTATIVE of illustrator and jewelry designer Wendy Wallin Malinow's whimsical style. The pins are colorful and full of sparkling inclusions suspended in pools of resin. Wear several on a jacket or use them to accent a scarf or handbag. Polymer clay comes in a variety of colors and can be mixed to any hue or shade imaginable. This project will open your mind to the many possibilities of combining polymer clay and resin to create your own colorful creations.

To make several pins, you will need:

2 ounces polymer clay or small amounts of different colors for multiple flowers (Sculpey III)

EasyCast clear casting epoxy

Transparent dye for tinting resin (optional; Castin'Craft)

Silver wires or head pins (three to five per pin)

Faceted crystal beads

Glass seed beads

Glitter

Glass rhinestones

Art Glitter glass glitter shards (Art Institute Glitter Inc.)

Micro Beedz™ (Art Accentz™)

Pin back finding

Devcon 2-Ton epoxy adhesive

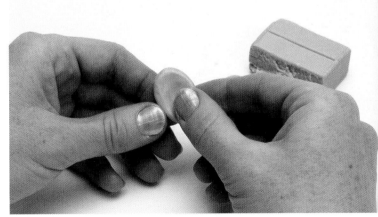

1. Read the section about polymer clay on page 108 for more information about working with polymer clay before beginning this project. Pinch off a small amount of polymer clay and condition it by kneading it with your hands until soft.

To make the petals for the flower, divide and roll the clay into six small balls (five for the petals and one for the center of the flower).

2. Begin to shape the petals by forming the balls of clay into flat oval shapes.

3. Sculpt the ovals into hollow "bowl" forms with your fingers.

4. Arrange the petals into a circle to form a flower, pressing the petals together at the bases to attach.

5. Push the remaining ball of clay into the center of the flower petals. Hollow the ball to make a "well" or "bowl" cavity in the clay.

6. Make "stamens" for the center of the flower. To do so, use pliers to bend the end of a piece of wire (or you can use head pins instead).

Thread a faceted crystal bead followed by three to four seed beads onto each wire. Clip the ends of the wires, leaving about ⅛ to ¼ inch wire exposed at the bottom. Make three to five pieces for the center of each flower.

7. Push the wires into the clay center of the flower. Don't worry about anchoring the wires securely at this step. The resin will hold them securely in place after the clay is baked.

8. Decorate the flower with bits of polymer clay or rhinestones pushed into the clay. Bake the finished flower in an oven at 275°F for 30 minutes, following manufacturer's instructions. Let the pieces cool in the oven.

9. Prepare a small batch of resin (about 20 cc). If you want to tint the resin, add a small amount of dye with a toothpick. The more color you use, the more opaque the resin will become; keep the resin transparent if you want to see the rhinestones in the bottoms of the petals.

Use a craft stick to fill the petals and the center of the flower. Stray drops of resin on the petals will sparkle like dew drops on the finished flower pins; you might want to add them intentionally.

10. Sprinkle glitter, Beedz, seed beads, glass shards, or other inclusions into the resin while it is still fluid. Use a toothpick to rearrange the inclusions if necessary.

Remove air bubbles in the resin by passing a heat gun over the surface. Let the resin sit in a warm place for 24 to 72 hours until fully cured.

Use epoxy to attach a pin back to the back of the flower to finish the pin.

Faux Dichroic Glass Pendant

DICHROIC GLASS IS LAYERED and then fused in a kiln to create beautiful iridescent patterns. Fine glitter and polymer clay are used to simulate the look of dichroic glass with simple materials and techniques. Resin enables you to work with unusually shaped bezels, which would be difficult with glass.

To make one necklace, you will need:

Purchased bezel (oval from Blue Moon Beads; square shape from Sherri Haab Designs)

Black polymer clay (Kato Polyclay)

Pasta machine

Waxed paper

Very fine glitter (Microfine Sparklerz Glitters™ by Art Accentz)

Pearl Ex powdered pigments (Jacquard)

Envirotex Lite epoxy resin

Chain for necklace

Project by Jacqueline Lee.

1. Condition clay according to package directions. Roll out a sheet of clay on the thinnest setting of the pasta machine and lay it on waxed paper. Because the clay is so thin, the waxed paper offers a nonstick surface that reduces the chances of tearing the clay.

Using your finger, apply a palette of glitters and powdered pigments to the clay. Don't be afraid to mix the colors.

2. Use a craft knife to cut small shapes out of the decorated clay and layer them into the bezel in any arrangement that you find pleasing. If you prefer, you can draw the bezel shape on paper, sketch out a design you like, and then cut it apart to make pattern pieces.

When your design is complete, place the decorated bezel in the oven and bake at 275°F for about 20 minutes. Let cool in the oven.

3. Mix a small amount of resin according to the manufacturer's instructions to coat the baked clay. This resin mixes with a ratio of 1:1. Use a craft stick or toothpick to move the resin to the edges of the bezel. Let the resin cure overnight or for several days in a warm place. Add a chain to finish the pendant.

Project by Jacqueline Lee.

Polymer Clay Collage Pendant

FOR THIS COLORFUL PENDANT, small seed beads, glitters, and powders are applied to textured polymer clay and then sealed with resin. Resin provides a coating to protect elements that would otherwise be difficult to apply to polymer clay. The depth of the resin enhances the texture of the clay and magnifies the sparkle of the elements.

To make one necklace, you will need:

Black and translucent polymer clay (Kato Polyclay)

Pasta machine

Silver leaf

Very fine glitter (Microfine Sparklerz Glitters by Art Accentz)

Chunky Sparklerz™ glitter (Art Accentz)

Black glitter

Gel pens

Deco Bollio™ rubber stamp (Judikins)

Seed beads

Bugle beads

Perfect Pearls™ pigment powders (Ranger)

White glue

Clear casting resin (EasyCast)

Square cutter (optional)

Epoxy resin adhesive (Devcon 2-Ton)

Plastic-coated wire

Cord for hanging pendant

1. Condition the polymer clays according to the package directions. Roll out a sheet of black clay on setting #3 (on a pasta roller for which #1 is the thickest setting). Spray the clay with water. Press the rubber stamp into the clay *very* firmly to emboss the clay.

2. Cut out a small rectangle of the embossed clay. Highlight some of the raised areas with the pigment powders. Embed seed beads and bugle beads into some areas of the design.

3. Roll out the thinnest sheet of translucent clay that you can easily handle and apply glitter to small pieces with your finger. Cut out tiny shapes and apply them to the piece as desired. Bake the piece at 275°F for 15 to 20 minutes.

4. After the piece has cooled, use the gel pens to accent some of the raised areas and then allow it to dry.

5. Mix a small batch of resin to coat the clay. A strip of cellophane tape around the edges will allow you to pour a thicker coating of resin. When the resin has hardened, remove the tape.

Drill a small hole in the pendant and glue a wire loop in place with epoxy adhesive. Attach a cord for hanging to finish the pendant.

Contributing Artists

The following artists have generously allowed me to show their work in this book (see pages 8 through 13) or contributed projects. Most of them have Web sites on which you can view more of their jewelry.

Robert Dancik
www.robertdancik.com

Carla Edwards
www.carlaedwards.co.uk

Charlie Hines
"Bedebug—Peculiar Objects and Specimen"
www.bedebug.com

Jacqueline Lee
www.jacquelineleeonline.com

Wendy Wallin Malinow
eyefun@comcast.net

Renathe Schneider
www.renathe.com

Lulu Smith
www.lulusmith.com

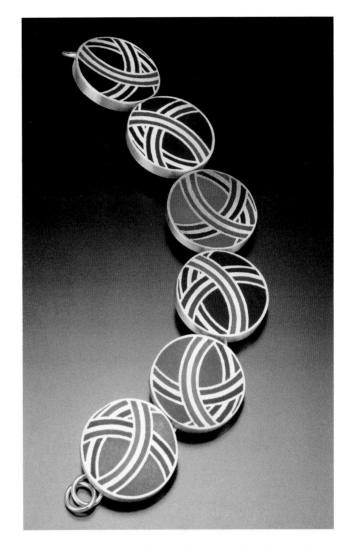

Yarn Bracelet by Lulu Smith. (Photo by Douglas Yaple.)

Mosaic Series Pin by Charlie Hines. (Photo by artist.)

Suppliers

Listed below are the manufacturers and suppliers of many of the materials used in this book. Most of these companies sell their products to retail and online stores. Contact these companies directly to find a retailer near you.

Alumilite Corporation
800-447-9344
www.alumilite.com
Casting resin, moldmaking rubber, and casting accessories

ARTchix Studio
250-370-9985
www.artchixstudio.com
Vintage collage sheets, charms, fasteners, and findings

Art Institute Glitter, Inc.
877-909-0905
www.artglitter.com
Art Glitter glass glitter shards

Artistic Wire
630-530-7567
www.artisticwire.com
Wire, tools, and kits

Aspen Art Stamps
801-491-7408
www.aspenartstamps.com
Vintage Milk Paints, unmounted rubber stamps, and collage sheets

Blue Moon Beads
800-377-6715
www.beads.net
Beads and findings

Cartwright's Sequins
479-369-2074
www.ccartwright.com
Sequins

Clay Factory, Inc.
877-728-5739
www.clayfactoryinc.com
Polymer clay, tools, and general supplies

DMD Industries, Inc.
800-805-9890
www.dmdind.com
Collage Papers™, card stock, and ribbon

Dover Publications
www.doverpublications.com
Clip art books and CD-ROMs

Eastern Findings
800-332-6640
www.easternfindings.com
Brass stampings, bezels, jewelry findings, and supplies

Environmental Technology, Inc. (ETI)
707-443-9323
www.eti-usa.com
Envirotex Lite® epoxy resin, EasyCast® casting epoxy, and Castin'Craft dyes, molds, and mold release spray

Fire Mountain Gems
800-355-2137
www.firemountaingems.com
Beads, findings, stringing supplies, and books

Halstead Bead, Inc.
800-528-0535
www.halsteadbead.com
Metal beads, findings, and wire

Harbor Freight Tools
800-444-3353
www.harborfreight.com
Hardware, tools, and metal punches

Jacquard Products/Rupert, Gibbon & Spider, Inc.
800-442-0455
www.jacquardproducts.com
Pearl Ex powdered pigments and paints

Jewelry Supply
916-780-9610
www.jewelrysupply.com
General jewelrymaking supplies and belt buckles

Junkitz™
732-792-1108
www.junkitz.com
Ringz jump rings

Karen Foster Designs
801-451-9779
www.karenfosterdesign.com
Build-A-Bezel embellishments

Kitchen Krafts
800-776-0575
www.kitchenkrafts.com
Guttman flexible candy molds

Magic Scraps
904-482-0092
www.magicscraps.com
Shaved Ice

Metalliferous, Inc.
888-944-0909
www.metalliferous.com
*Jewelry findings, brass stampings
wire, tools, and supplies*

Michael Miller Memories
646-230-8862
www.michaelmiller
memories.com
Fabric paper

National Artcraft Co.
888-937-2723
www.nationalartcraft.com
*Art and craft supplies, crushed
glass, glitter, pastels*

Nature's Pressed
800-850-2499
www.naturespressed.com
Pressed flowers and leaves

Plaid Enterprises, Inc.
800-842-4197
www.plaidonline.com
Mod Podge® decoupage glue

Polyform Products Co.
847-427-0020
www.sculpey.com
*Sculpey™ and Premo™ clay
products*

Polymer Clay Express
800-844-0138
www.polymerclayexpress.com
*Polymer clay, clay shapers, blades
and clay cutters, findings, and
tools*

Prairie Craft Company
800-779-0615
www.prairiecraft.com
*Kato Polyclay™ polymer clay and
Kato clear liquid medium*

Provo Craft
800-937-7686
www.provocraft.com
*Art Accentz™ Beedz™ and
Microfine Sparklerz Glitter™*

Prym-Dritz Corporation
www.dritz.com
*Fray-Check™ sealant, eyelets, and
sewing and craft supplies*

Ranger Industries, Inc.
800-244-2211
www.rangerink.com
*Perfect Pearls™, rubber stamping
supplies, and Suze Weinberg's
embellishments*

Rio Grande®
800-545-6566
www.riogrande.com
*Colores™ epoxy resin, Belicone®
silicone rubber putty, jewelry
findings, and general supplies*

Sherri Haab Designs
801-489-3885
www.sherrihaab.com
*Handmade charms and bezels,
craft kits, and resin molds*

Smooth-On, Inc.
800-762-0744
www.smooth-on.com
*Smooth-Cast™ polyurethane resin,
OOMOO™ silicone rubber, So-
Strong™ tints, casting supplies
and accessories, and videos and
workshops*

Soft Flex Company
707-938-3539
www.softflexcompany.com
Soft Flex® wire

Sugarcraft™
513-896-7089
www.sugarcraft.com
Guttman flexible candy molds

Therm O Web
847-520-5200
www.thermoweb.com
*HeatnBond® iron-on adhesives
and PEELnSTICK™ double-sided
adhesive sheets and tape*

The Vintage Workshop®
913-341-5559
www.thevintageworkshop.com
*Click-n-Craft® CD-ROMs and
downloadable art*

Yaley Enterprises, Inc.
800-959-2539
www.yaley.com
*Deep Flex™ molds, resin, and
supplies*

Index

Air bubbles, 23, 65, 72, 82, 115
Amber, 101
  faux, 101–105

Bakelite-style bracelet, 50–51
Bangle bracelets, 97–100
Barrier cream, 19
Beads
  adding sparkle to, 71–73
  adding, to head pins, 45
  pod bead bracelet, 89–91
Bead tips, 32
Belt buckle, sequined, 109–111
Bezels, 108
  polymer clay, 113–115
Bracelets
  Bakelite-style, 50–51
  bangle, 97–100
  fabric stretch, 58
  faux celluloid, 83–86
  photo collage charm, 43–44
  pod bead, 89–91
  pressed flower, 37–38
  retro stretch, 63–65
  silver or gold leaf, 59–61
Brooch, heart, 52. See also Pins

Candy jewelry, 74–76
Carnelian necklace, faux, 95
Celluloid, 83
  faux, 83–86
Charm bracelet, photo collage, 43–44
Clasps, 32
Cloisonné-style jewelry, 41–42
Color
  adding, 25–26
  formulas for faux amber, 105
Crimp beads, 32
Curing
  polymer clay and, 108
  resin, 23, 49

Dancik, Robert, 12, 126
Dichroic glass, 120
Drilling, 29
Dust mask, 20

Earrings
  faux amber, 105
  flower, 39
  rose, 86–87
Ear wires, 31
Edwards, Carla, 9, 126
Epoxy resin, 16–17
Eye goggles, 20
Eye pins, 31

Fabric
  pendant, 55–56
  rings, 57
  stretch bracelet, 58
Fillers, 27
Findings, 31–32
Flower bracelet, 37–38

Glasses, protective, 20
Gold leaf, 62

Head pins, 31
  adding beads to, 45
Hines, Charlie, 9, 126

Inclusions, 27, 71–73, 97

Jade neckpiece, faux, 93–94
Jewelrymaking
  findings, 31–32
  suppliers, 128–129
  tools, 30
  wrapping wire loops, 33
Jump rings, 31, 32

Lee, Jacqueline, 120, 122, 126
Liquid latex, 81

Malinow, Wendy Wallin, 11, 13, 18, 117, 126
Material Safety Data Sheet (MSDS), 19
Measuring resin, 22
Mixing resin, 22
Molds, 72, 75. See also Release agents
  determining volume for, 82
  making your own, 80–82
  polymer clay and, 108
  materials for, 81–82

working with preformed, 48–53
National Institute for Occupational Safety and Health (NIOSH), 19
Necklaces
  faux carnelian, 95
  faux jade, 93–94
  glitter gem bead, 71–73
  gold leaf, 62
  with polymer clay, 113–115

Pendants
  fabric, 55–56
  faux dichroic glass, 120–121
  heart, 77
  polymer clay bezel, 113–115
  polymer clay collage, 123–125
  rose, 86–87
Pin backs, 32
Pins
  funky flower, 117–119
  gold leaf, 62
  scatter, 53
Polyester casting resin, 18
Polymer clay, 108
  bezels, techno, 113–115
  collage pendant, 123–125
  combining resin and, 117–119
  faux dichroic glass, 120–121
  funky flower pins, 117–119
  sequined belt buckle, 109–111
Polyurethane casting resin, 17–18
Polyurethane rubber molds, 82
Pressed flower bracelet, 37–38

Release agents, 48–49, 75
Resin
  adding color to, 25–26
  adding three-dimensional elements to, 68
  casting three-dimensional forms, 48–53
  characteristics of, 9–10

combining polymer clay and, 117–119
  curing, 23
  epoxy, 16–17
  finishing techniques, 28–29
  history of, 9
  measuring and mixing techniques, 22
  mix-ins, 27. See also Inclusions
  polyester, 18
  polyurethane, 17–18
  predecessors to modern, 10–11
  removing air bubbles from, 23
  safety guidelines and equipment, 19–20
  setting up working environment for, 21
  supplies, 21
  types of, 16–18
Respirator, 19
Rings
  fabric, 57
  penny candy, 76
Room-temperature-vulcanizing (RTV) molds, 81

Safety
  equipment, 19–20
  measures, 19
  moldmaking, 80
Sanding
  polymer clay, 108
  resin, 28
Schneider, Renathe, 10, 11, 126
Silicone putty mold compounds, 82
Silicone rubber, 81–82
Silver leaf, 59–62
Smith, Lulu, 8, 11, 126, 127
Suppliers, jewelrymaking, 128–129

Tools, jewelrymaking, 30

Wire wrapping, 33
Work area, setting up, 21